Guiding Those Left Behind In Maryland

LEGAL AND PRACTICAL THINGS
YOU NEED TO DO
TO SETTLE AN ESTATE IN MARYLAND
and
HOW TO ARRANGE YOUR OWN AFFAIRS
TO AVOID UNNECESSARY COSTS
TO YOUR FAMILY

By AMELIA E. POHL, ESQ.

with Maryland Attorney
KEVIN F. BRESS

EAGLE PUBLISHING COMPANY OF BOCA

The purpose of this book is to provide the reader with an accurate and informative overview of the subject but laws change frequently and are subject to different interpretations as courts rule on the meaning or effect of a law. This book is sold with the understanding that neither the publisher nor the authors are engaging in, nor rendering legal, medical, psychiatric, accounting, financial planning, or any other professional service. If you need legal, accounting, financial planning, medical, psychiatric or other expert advice, then you should seek the services of a licensed professional.

WEB SITES: Web sites appear throughout the book. These Web sites are offered for the convenience of the reader only. Publication of these Web site addresses is not an endorsement by the authors, editors or publishers of this book.

This book is intended for use by the consumer for his or her own benefit. If you use this book to counsel someone about the law, accounting or medicine, then that may be considered an unauthorized and illegal practice.

EAGLE PUBLISHING COMPANY OF BOCA
4199 N. Dixie Highway, #2
Boca Raton, FL 33431
E-mail info@eaglepublishing.com

Printed in the United States of America
ISBN 1-892407-45-0
Library of Congress Catalog Card Number: 2001089973

The Organization of the Book

If you are going to GUIDE THOSE LEFT BEHIND, you need to know what is involved in settling an estate in Maryland, so we begin the book explaining that process. The first six chapters explain:

1. How to tend to the funeral and burial
2. What agencies need to be notified of the death
3. How to locate the decedent's property
4. What bills need (and do not need) to be paid
5. Determining who are the beneficiaries
6. Getting the decedent's property to the proper beneficiary

We devoted a chapter to each of these 6 steps; and for those who are in the process of settling an estate, we placed a CHECK LIST at the end of Chapter 6 summarizing the many things that need to be done.

Once you read Chapters 1 through 6 you will be able to identify those problems that can occur when someone dies. Using those Chapters as a base, the rest of the book (Chapters 7 through 11) explain how you can set up your own Estate Plan so that your family is not burdened by similar problems.

GLOSSARY

This book is designed for the average reader. Legal terminology has been kept to a minimum. There is a glossary at the end of the book in the event you come across a legal term that is not familiar to you.

FICTITIOUS NAMES AND EVENTS

The examples in this book are based loosely on actual events; however, all names are fictitious; and the events, as portrayed, are fictitious.

ACKNOWLEDGMENT

When someone dies, the family attorney is often among the first to be called. Family members have questions about whether probate is necessary, who to notify, how to get possession of the assets, etc. Over the years, as we practiced in the field of Elder Law, we noticed that the questions raised were much the same family to family. We both agreed that a book answering such questions would be of service to the general public.

We also observed, that those who had experience in settling the estate of a loved one had an understanding of the process, and were better able to make decisions about their own estate plan. We decided to combine the two topics: Settling An Estate and Estate Planning into a single book ***Guiding Those Left Behind***. We wish to thank all of the clients, whom we have had the honor and pleasure to serve, for providing us with the impetus to produce this book.

SPECIAL THANKS FROM AMELIA E. POHL

I wish to thank my brothers Paul and Fred Adinolfi, my sister Nancy Simonyi, my daughters Louise Lucas and Margo Bosche, and my husband J. William Pohl. Working on this series of books was just that much easier because of the support given to me by all the members of my family.

SPECIAL THANKS FROM KEVIN F. BRESS

To my wife and daughters who have unselfishly encouraged me to complete this project, I love and appreciate them. And to my parents who taught me how to write, I am grateful.

About The Author

Before becoming an attorney in 1985, AMELIA E. POHL taught mathematics on both the high school and college level. During her tenure as Associate Professor of Mathematics at Prince George's Community College in Maryland, she wrote several books including Probability: A Set Theory Approach, Principals of Counting and Common Stock Sense.

During her practice of law Attorney Pohl observed that many people want to reduce the high cost of legal fees by performing or assisting with their own legal transactions. Attorney Pohl found that, with a bit of guidance, people are able to perform many legal transactions for themselves. Attorney Pohl utilizes her background as teacher, author and attorney to provide that "bit of guidance" to the general public in the form of self-help legal books that she has written. Attorney Pohl is currently "translating" this book for the remaining 49 states:

Guiding Those Left Behind in Alabama

Guiding Those Left Behind in Connecticut, etc.

Consulting Maryland Attorney

KEVIN F. BRESS, ESQ., manages the Trust, Estate and Elder Law Departments for the Maryland law firm of Hodes, Ulman, Pessin & Katz, P.A. Mr. Bress received his Juris Doctor and Masters of Science in Taxation degrees from the University of Baltimore in 1984. He is an adjunct professor at the University of Baltimore School of Law Graduate Tax Program and has taught Elder Law for Villa Julie College. He has testified on tax law issues as an expert witness in legal matters before the district court.

His community service includes serving as counsel to the Boys and Girls Club of Harford County, and Mr. Bress has previously been active with the local Alzheimers Association chapter.

Mr. Bress has lectured extensively throughout Maryland on estates, trusts and Elder Law topics, including presentations to attorneys, accountants, health care professionals and financial advisors for their continuing education requirements. He is a member of the National Academy of Elder Law Attorneys and is a member of both the Elder Law Section and Trust and Estate Section of the Maryland State Bar Association.

The law firm of Hodes, Ulman Pessin and Katz is one of the preeminent Maryland law firms that concentrates in both estate planning and Elder Law matters. With 18 of the firm's 47 attorneys experienced in estate, trust, tax and Elder Law, the firm has helped thousands of families deal with these issues.

The firm is equipped to deal with such complex matters as probate for farm estates, charitable trusts, filing estate and gift tax returns, wealth preservation, drafting wills, powers of attorney and advance directives. In addition, the firm's Elder Law practice encompasses Medicaid Planning, guardianship and asset protection for seniors. Mr. Bress regularly conducts free, informative seminars on these topics, and the readers are invited to call to the law firm to sign up for Mr. Bress' presentations at (410) 938-8800.

Hodes, Ulman, Pessin & Katz has offices in Towson, Bel Air, Columbia, and Cambridge, Maryland. You can learn more about the firm by visiting their Web site at http://www.hupk.com. Mr. Bress invites comments and questions from the readers to be sent to his e-mail address: KBress@hupk.com

Guiding Those Left Behind In Maryland

CONTENTS

Reading the Law

Where applicable, we identified the Maryland statute or federal statute that is the basis of the discussion. We did this as a reference, and also to encourage the general public to read the law as it is written. Prior to the Internet the only way you could look up the law was to physically take yourself to the local courthouse law library or the law section of a public library. Today all of the state and federal statutes are literally at your finger tips. They are just a mouse click away on the Internet. To look up the law all you need is the address of the Web site and the identifying number of the statute. All of the federal statutes are available at the following Web site.

FEDERAL STATUTE WEB SITE
http://www4.law.cornell.edu/uscode

Looking up the Maryland statute is more of a challenge but you can find the statutes by using your search engine. For example, you can go to the Findlaw site:

http://www.findlaw.com

Once at the site go to Laws: Cases and Codes. From there scroll down to Maryland. And from there to State Code. Maryland statutes are divided into some 101 Articles. We will identify the law by the number of its Article and section within the Article; for example (MC 27-819) refers to section 819 of Article 27 of the Maryland Code. In addition to the 101 numbered Articles there are Articles that have names instead of numbers, such as "Estates and Trusts" "Tax-General" "Insurance" "Health-General" "Courts and Judicial Proceedings," etc. For those statutes we will name the Article; for example (Est.& Trusts 1-203) refers to section 1-203 of the Estates and Trusts Article.

If you come across a topic that is of importance to you, then you may find it both interesting and profitable to read the law as it is written.

About The Book

We tried to make this book as comprehensive as possible so there are specialized sections of the book that do not apply to the general population and may not be of interest to you. The following GUIDE POSTS appear throughout the book. You can read the section if the situation applies to you or skip the section if it doesn't.

GUIDE POSTS

SPOUSE

The SPOUSE POST means that the information provided is specifically for the spouse of the decedent. If the decedent was single, then skip this section.

LAWYER

The CALL-A-LAWYER POST alerts you to a situation that may require the assistance of an attorney. See page xiii for information about how to find a lawyer.

CAUTION

The CAUTION POST alerts you to a potential problem. It is followed by a suggestion about how to avoid the problem.

Special Situation

The SPECIAL SITUATION POST means that the information given in that paragraph applies to a particular event or situation; for example when someone dies a violent death. If the situation does not apply in your case then you can skip the section.

When You Need A Lawyer

The purpose of the book is to give the reader a basic understanding of what needs to be done when someone dies, and to provide information about how a person can arrange his own affairs to avoid problems for his own family. It is not intended as a substitute for legal counsel or any other kind of professional advice. If you have any legal question, then you should to seek the counsel of an attorney. When looking for an attorney, consider three things: EXPERTISE, COST and PERSONALITY.

EXPERTISE

The state of Maryland does not have a program to certify that an attorney is specialized in a particular area of law. This being the case an attorney in Maryland may not represent to the public that he/she is a "specialist" in any given area of law. Attorneys are allowed to state that they concentrate on certain areas of law. Before employing an attorney for a job, ask how long he has practiced that type of law and what percentage of his practice is devoted to that type of law. The Maryland State Bar Association, Inc. can refer you to an attorney for who practices the type of law that you seek. You can call them (800) 492-1964 or visit their Web site for the telephone number of the Lawyer Referral Service nearest you:

MARYLAND STATE BAR ASSOCIATION, INC.
http:// www.msba.org/

One of the most reliable ways of finding an attorney is through personal referral. Ask your friends, family or business acquaintances if they used an attorney for the field of law that you seek and whether they were pleased with the results. It is important to employ an attorney who is experienced in the area of law you seek. Your friend may have a wonderful Estate Planning attorney, but if you suffered an injury to your body, you need an attorney who is experienced in Personal Injury.

Before employing an attorney for a job, ask how long he has practiced that type of law and what percentage of his practice is devoted to that type of law.

COST

In addition to the attorney's experience, it is important to check what it will cost in attorney's fees. When you call for an appointment ask what the attorney will charge for the initial consultation and the approximate cost for the service you seek. Ask whether there will be additional costs such as filing fees, accounting fees, expert witness fees, etc.

If the least expensive attorney is out of your price range then the PRO BONO RESOURCE CENTER OF MARYLAND can refer you to an attorney in you area. This organization was established by the Maryland State Bar Association together with the Maryland Legal Services Corporation, the Maryland Bar Foundation and the Court of Appeals of Maryland to provide civil legal assistance to people of low income. You can reach the Resource Center by calling the Maryland Bar at (800) 492-1964.

The American Bar Association has a directory of Maryland Legal Services Programs at the General Public Resources section of its Web Site:

AMERICAN BAR ASSOCIATION WEB SITE

htttp://www.abanet.org

PERSONALITY

Of equal importance to the attorney's experience and legal fees, is your relationship with the attorney. How easy was it to reach the attorney? Did you go through layers of receptionists and legal assistants before being allowed to speak to the attorney? Did the attorney promptly return your call? If you had difficulty reaching the attorney, then you can expect similar problems should you employ that attorney.

Did the attorney treat you with respect? Did the attorney treat you paternally with a "father knows best" attitude or did the attorney treat you as an intelligent person with the ability to understand the options available to you and the ability to make your own decision based on the information provided to you.

Are you able to understand and easily communicate with the attorney? Is he/she speaking to you in plain English or is his/her explanation of the matter so full of legalese to be meaningless to you?

Do you find the attorney's personality to be pleasant or grating? Sometimes people rub each other the wrong way. It is like rubbing a cat the wrong way. Stroking a cat from head to tail is pleasing to the cat, but petting it in the opposite direction, no matter how well intended, causes friction. If the lawyer makes you feel annoyed or uncomfortable, then find another attorney.

It is worth the effort to take the time to interview as many attorneys as it takes to find one with the right expertise, fee schedule and personality for you.

The First Week 1

Dealing with the death of a close family member or friend is difficult. Not only do you need to deal with your own emotions, but often with those of your family and friends. Sometimes their sorrow is more painful to you, than what you are experiencing yourself.

In addition to the emotional impact of a death, there are many things that need to be done, from arranging the funeral and burial, to closing out the business affairs of the ***decedent*** (the person who died) and finally giving whatever property is left to the proper beneficiary.

The funeral and burial take only a few days. Wrapping up the affairs of the decedent may take considerably longer. This chapter explains what things you (the spouse or closest family member) need to do during the first week, beginning at the moment of death and continuing through the funeral.

> ♀ MALE GENDER USED ♂
>
> Rather than use "he/she" or "his/her" for simplicity (and hoping not to offend anyone) we will refer to the decedent and his Personal Representative using the male gender.
>
> References to other people will be in both genders.

AUTOPSIES

In today's high tech world of medicine, doctors are fairly certain of the cause of death, but if there is a question, the doctor may seek permission to perform an autopsy. Consent may be given by the decedent's parent, spouse, child, guardian, next of kin or any other person who has control of the body for its final disposition. Consent should be in writing, however a telegram or a recorded message is sufficient to give authority for the examination (Health-Gen 5-501).

The person giving authorization must agree to pay for the autopsy because the cost is not covered under most health insurance plans. The cost of an autopsy can run anywhere from several hundred to well over three thousand dollars, but it is in the family's best interest to consent to the autopsy. The examination might reveal a genetic disorder, that could be treated if it later appears in another family member. Death from a car "accident" could have been a heart attack at the wheel. Perhaps the patient who died suddenly in a hospital was misdiagnosed. The nursing home resident could have died from negligence and not old age. Even if none of these are found, knowing the cause of death with certainty is better than not knowing.

That was the case with the family of a woman who was taken to the hospital complaining of stomach pains. The doctors thought she might be suffering from gallbladder disease but she died before they could effectively treat her. A doctor suggested that an autopsy be performed to determine the actual cause of death. The woman had three daughters, one of whom objected to the autopsy:

"Why spend that kind of money?
It won't bring Mom back."

The daughter's wishes were respected, however over the years as they aged and became ill with their own various ailments they would undergo physical examinations. As part of taking their medical history, doctors routinely asked "And what was the cause of your mother's death?" None could answer the question.

This is not a dramatic story. No mysterious genetic disorder ever occurred in any of her daughters, nor in any of their children. But each daughter (including the one who objected) at some point in her life, was confronted with the nagging question "What did Mom die of?"

MANDATORY AUTOPSIES

When a person dies, a physician must sign the death certificate stating the cause of death. For those who die in a hospital there is a doctor present to sign the certificate. If a person who was not under the care of a physician, dies suddenly at home, or if someone dies through accident, foul play or suicide, then the police must be notified. The person who discovers the body should call 911 to summon the police. The police will ask the medical examiner to determine the cause of death. If there is a suspicion that the death was not from natural causes or if the decedent died from a disease that might pose a threat to the public health, then the Chief Medical Examiner will authorize a qualified person to perform the autopsy (Health-Gen 5-309, 5-310).

AUTOPSIES PERFORMED BY THE INSURANCE COMPANY:

Any company that issues a health insurance policy in the state of Maryland must include a provision in their policy giving the company the right to conduct an autopsy (Insur. 15-216). The cost of the autopsy is paid for by the insurance company, so they will not do so unless there is some good reason for the examination.

ANATOMICAL GIFTS

If, before death, the decedent made an anatomical gift by signing a donor card or by giving his Health Care Agent authority to make the gift as part of a Durable Power of Attorney For Health Care, then hospital personnel or the donor's doctor need to be made aware of the gift in quick proximity to the time of death — preferably before death.

GIFT AUTHORIZED BY THE FAMILY

Hospital personnel determine whether a mortally ill patient is a candidate for an organ donation. Early on in the donor program those over 65 were not considered as suitable candidates. Today, however, the condition of the organ, and not the age, is the determining factor.

The federal government has established regional Organ Procurement Organizations throughout the United States to coordinate the donor program. The Organ Procurement Organization for Maryland is located in Baltimore. It is called THE TRANSPLANT RESOURCE CENTER OF MARYLAND. If it is determined that a patient may be a candidate for a donation, the hospital will contact the Transplant Resource Center. The Transplant. Resource Center will determine whether the patient is a suitable donor. If they decide to request the gift and the candidate did not sign a donor card, then someone in the family must give written permission. Someone who is specially trained will approach the family to request the donation. Maryland statute establishes an order of priority to authorize the donation:

- 1st Spouse
- 2nd Adult son or daughter
- 3rd Either parent
- 4th Adult brother or sister
- 5th The court appointed guardian of the decedent
- 6th Any other person or agency authorized to dispose of the body.

If permission is obtained from a family member and there are others in the same or a higher priority, then an effort must be made to contact those people and make them aware of the proposed gift. For example, if the sister of the decedent agrees to the gift (4th in priority) and the decedent had an adult child (2nd in priority), then the child needs to be made aware of the gift. If the child objects, then no gift can be made. Similarly, the statute prohibits the gift if the decedent ever expressed his opposition to a donation (Estates & Trusts 4-503).

AFTER THE DONATION

Once the donation is made the body is delivered to the funeral home and prepared for burial or cremation as directed by the family. The donation does not disfigure the body so there can be an open casket viewing if the family so wishes.

For privacy reasons, the identity of the donor and the recipient of the gift is not disclosed, but on request from the donor's or recipient's family, most Organ Procurement Organizations will give basic demographic information such as the age, sex, marital status, number of children and occupation of the donor or recipient of the gift.

GIFT FOR EDUCATION OR RESEARCH

If the decedent signed a donor card indicating his wish to use his body for any purpose and he is not a candidate for an organ donation, then you can offer to release the body to be used for education or research. The Anatomy Board of Maryland coordinates the donation and arranges to have the body transported to a medical or research facility in Maryland. You will first need to call to determine whether they will accept the body. Most schools do not accept bodies from those who have died from a contagious disease or from crushing injuries or who were seriously obese.

Anatomy Board of Maryland
655 West Baltimore Street, Room B-026
Baltimore, MD 21201
Telephone: (410) 706-3313

There is also a federal program within the state of Maryland that accepts donations to be used in the Federal Medical Schools. They accept donations from within 150 miles of the nation's capital.

UNIFORMED SERVICES UNIVERSITY
4301 Jones Bridge Road
Bethesda, MD 20814-4799
Telephone: (301) 295-3333

If either of these agencies accept the donation, then there is no cost to the family either to transport the body to the school, or for the final disposition of the body.

The study usually takes from 18 months to 2 years. Once the study is complete the remains are cremated. If the family wishes the ***cremains*** (cremated remains) will be returned to the family. If the family does not wish the cremains returned, they are buried at a local site.

CAVEAT: It is illegal for anyone to purchase body parts (Health-Gen. 5-408). It is legal to charge monies to prepare or transport bodies or body parts. Not-for profit and as well as for-profit companies have sprung up that are in the business of preparing and delivering body parts. These companies request donations from families (so they are not buying body parts). The company prepares the body tissue or other parts of the body, and then distributes the parts throughout the United States to physicians, hospitals, research centers, etc.

In many cases the monies charged for preparation and transportation includes a sizable profit. If someone other than your local Organ Procurement Organization (The Transplant Resource Center of Maryland) approaches you to make a donation, then before making the donation you may want to learn about the company requesting the donation.

What is the name of the company?
Where are their main headquarters located?
What is their primary business activity?
What is the name and job description of the person making the request?

DETERMINE THE END USE OF THE DONATION

You may want to ask what they intend to do with the tissue or body part. If it is being used for research, then what type of research? Where is the research being conducted? If it will be used for transplantation, then what agency (doctor, hospital) will receive the donation and where is that agency located?

Once you have this information you can make an informed decision as to whether you wish to make the donation.

THE FUNERAL

Approximately ten percent of deaths occur suddenly because of accident, suicide, foul play or undetected illness. But, mostly, death occurs after a lengthy illness, with a common scenario being that of an aged person who dies after being ill for several months, if not years. In such case, family and friends are emotionally prepared for the happening. Expected or not, the first job is the disposition of the body.

THE PREARRANGED FUNERAL

Increasingly, people are arranging, in advance, for their own funeral and burial. This makes it easier on the family both financially and emotionally. All the decisions have been made and there is no guessing what the decedent would have wanted.

If the decedent made provision for his burial, then you should come across a burial certificate, or perhaps a deed to a burial space. If he made provision for his funeral, then you should find a Preneed funeral contract. You need to read the contract to determine what provisions were made. If the contract was paid on by installment, then you need to determine whether it is paid in full. You also need to determine whether the contract was a fixed price agreement or whether there could be additional charges.

If you cannot locate the contract, but you know the decedent made provision for his funeral, then call the funeral home and ask them to send you a copy of the contract. If you believe the decedent purchased a funeral plan but you do not know the name of the funeral home, then call the local funeral homes. Many local funeral homes are owned by national firms with computer capacity to identify people who have purchased a contract in any of their many locations.

Once you have possession of the contract, take it with you to the funeral home and go over the terms of the contract with the funeral director. Inquire whether there is any charge that is not included in the contract.

MAKING FUNERAL ARRANGEMENTS

If the decedent died unexpectedly or without having made any prior funeral arrangements then your first job is to choose a funeral director and make arrangements for the funeral or cremation. Most people choose the nearest or most conveniently located funeral home without comparison shopping. However prices for these services can vary significantly from funeral home to funeral home. Savings can be had if you take the time to make a few phone calls.

Receiving price quotes by telephone is your right under Federal law. Federal Trade Commission ("FTC") Rule 453.2 (b) (1) requires a funeral director to give an accurate telephone quote of the prices of his goods and services. Funeral homes are listed in the telephone directory under FUNERAL DIRECTORS. If you live in a small town, there may be only one or two listings. If such is the case, then check out some funeral homes in the next largest city.

Funeral directors usually provide the following services:

- arrange for the transportation of the body to the funeral home and then to the burial site
- obtain burial transit permits
- arrange for the embalming or cremation of the body
- arrange funeral and memorial services and the viewing of the body
- obtain information for the death certificate
- order copies of the death certificate for the family
- have memorial cards printed.

To compare prices you will need to determine:

- what is included in the price of a basic funeral plan
- whether you can expect any additional cost.

If the decedent did not own a burial space, then that cost must be included when making funeral arrangements.

It may be necessary to have the body embalmed if you are going to have a viewing. Embalming is not necessary if you order a direct cremation or an immediate burial without a viewing. Federal Trade Commission Rule 453.5 prohibits the funeral home from charging an embalming fee unless you order the service.

PURCHASING THE CASKET

When comparison-shopping, you will find that the single most expensive item is the casket. When selecting a casket you need to be aware that there may be a considerable mark-up in the price quoted by the funeral director. You do not need to go "sole source" when purchasing the casket. If you feel that the price quoted by the funeral director is too high, you can purchase the casket elsewhere and have it delivered to the funeral home to be used instead of the one offered by the funeral director. Federal regulations require a funeral home to accept a casket that is purchased elsewhere.

The funeral director must provide you with a written price list at the beginning of your discussion of funeral arrangements. If the price list given to you by the funeral home states that the price of their casket includes a specific dollar amount for basic services, and you do not purchase the casket from the funeral home, then the funeral director is allowed to add that specific dollar amount to the charge for his basic services. He is not allowed to charge a handling fee for accepting a casket that is purchased elsewhere (FTC Rule 453.2, 453.4).

Of course the problem with purchasing a casket is that most of us have no idea what to pay. Caskets are not usually displayed for sale in a shopping mall, so how do you determine the going price? The answer is the Internet. You can learn all about the cost of any item, even a casket, by using your search engine to find a retail casket sales dealer. If you are not computer literate, you can locate the nearest retail casket sales outlet by looking in the yellow pages under CASKETS. You may need to look in the telephone directory for the nearest large city to find a listing. By making a call to a retail casket sales dealer, you will become knowledgeable in the price range of caskets. You can then decide what is a reasonable price for the product you seek.

The best time to do your comparison shopping, is before you go to the funeral home to arrange for the funeral. Once you have determined what you should pay for the casket, it is only fair to give the funeral director the opportunity to meet that price. If you cannot reach a meeting of the minds, then you can always order the casket from the retail sales dealer and have it delivered to the funeral home.

ON-LINE FUNERAL SERVICES

The Internet is changing the way the world does business, and the funeral industry is no exception. A growing number of mortuaries are offering live Webcasts of funerals and wakes for those who are unable to pay their respects in person.

There are Web sites such as ObitDetails.com where you can post an obituary. There are on-line memorial chat rooms as well as online eulogies and testimonials. There is even a Web site that offers a posthumous e-mail service which allows people to leave final messages for friends and relatives.

THE CREMATION

Increasingly people are opting for cremation. The reasons for choosing cremation are varied, but for the majority, it is a matter of finances. The cost of cremation is approximately one-sixth that of an ordinary funeral and burial. A major saving is the cost of the casket. No casket is necessary for the cremation. Federal and state law prohibit a Funeral Director from saying that a casket is required for a direct cremation (FTC Rule 453.3 (b)ii, Health Occup. 7-505). You may need a suitable container to deliver the body to the crematory. After the cremation, you may need an urn for the ashes.

If you are having a memorial service in a place of worship and no viewing of the body before the cremation, then consider contracting with a facility that does cremations only. Look in the telephone book CREMATION SERVICES. You will also see cremation "societies" in the telephone book. Some are for-profit and others non-profit. You can also find advertisements for cremation services on the Internet.

THE OVERWEIGHT DECEDENT

If the decedent weighs more than 300 pounds, then you need to check to see if the Cremation service has facilities large enough to handle the body. If you cannot locate a crematory that can accommodate the body, then you will need to make burial arrangements.

THE DECEDENT WITH A PACEMAKER

If the decedent was wearing a pacemaker or other electronic device, then you need to investigate the cost of removing the instrument prior to the cremation. Cremating a body with such devices can cause damage to the cremation chamber or to the person performing the cremation. The Cremation service may be able help you to arrange for the removal of the device.

DISPOSING OF THE ASHES

The decedent's cremains can be placed in a cemetery. Many cemeteries have a separate building called a ***columbarium***, which is especially designed to store urns. If not, then the cremains can be placed in a cemetery plot.

Some cemeteries allow the cremains of a family member to be placed in a occupied family plot. Similarly, some cemeteries allow the cremains to be placed in the space in a mausoleum that is currently occupied by a member of the decedent's family. If it is your desire to have the cremains placed in an occupied mausoleum or family plot, then you need to call the cemetery and ask them to explain their policy as it relates to the burial of urns in occupied sites.

If the cremains are to be placed in a cemetery, then you need to obtain a suitable urn for the burial. You can purchase the urn from the Funeral Director or Crematory Service Director. Urns cost much less than caskets, but they can cost several hundred dollars. You may wish to do some comparison shopping by calling a retail sales casket dealer.

The decedent may have expressed a desire that his ashes be spread out to sea. The Funeral Director or Cremation Service Director can assist you with such arrangements.

Special Situation

THE OUT OF STATE BURIAL

If the decedent is to be buried in another state, then the body will need to be transported to that state. Most funeral homes belong to a national network of funeral homes, and the out-of-state Funeral Director has the means to make local arrangements to ship the body. Contact the out-of-state Funeral Director and have him/her make arrangement with the airline for the transportation of the body. If services are to be held in Maryland and in another state, then your the local funeral director can make arrangements with the out-of-state funeral home for the transportation of the body.

If the body has been cremated, then you can transport the cremains yourself, either by carrying the ashes as part of your luggage or by arranging with the airline to transport the ashes as cargo. Have a certified copy of the death certificate available in the event that you need to identify the remains of the decedent. Call the airline before departure and ask whether they have any special regulation or procedure regarding the transportation of human ashes.

SPOUSE — THE MILITARY BURIAL

Subject to availability of burial spaces, an honorably discharged veteran and/or his unmarried minor or handicapped child and/or his un-remarried spouse may be buried in a Veterans cemetery. Some cemeteries have room only for cremated remains or for the casketed remains of a family member of someone who is currently buried in that cemetery, so you will need to call to check for space availability:

Annapolis National Cemetery; Annapolis, MD 21401
Baltimore National Cemetery; Baltimore, MD 21228
Loudon Park National Cemetery; Baltimore, MD 21228

For information on these national Veterans cemeteries call (410) 644-9696.

There are five state Veterans cemeteries in Maryland:

Cheltenham Veterans Cemetery.; Cheltenham, MD 20623
Crownsville Veterans Cemetery; Crownsville, MD 21032
Eastern Shore Veterans Cemetery; Hurlock, MD 21643
Garrison Forest Vet. Cemetery; Ownings Mills, MD 21117
Rocky Gap Veterans Cemetery; Flintstone, MD 21530

For information on these state Veterans cemeteries call the Maryland State Veterans Cemeteries at (410) 962-4700.

The Department of the Army is in charge of the Arlington National Cemetery. If you wish to have an eligible deceased veteran buried in the Arlington National Cemetery, then call them at (703) 695-3250.

Arlington National Cemetery
Interment Service Branch

Special Situation

THE COST OF A MILITARY BURIAL

Burial space in a National Cemetery is free of charge. Cemetery employees will open and close the grave and mark it with headstone or grave marker without cost to the family. The local Veteran's Administration ("VA") will provide the family with a memorial flag. The family needs to make funeral arrangements with a funeral firm and have them transport the remains to the cemetery.

Regardless of where a veteran, who was honorably discharged, is buried, there may be allowances available for plot, burial and grave marker expenses. The amount varies depending on factors such as whether the veteran died because of a service related injury. The VA will not reimburse any burial or funeral expense for the spouse of a veteran.

For information about reimbursement of funeral and burial expenses you can call the VA at (800) 827-1000.

The Department of Veteran's Affairs has a Web site with information on the following topics:

- National and Military Cemeteries
- Burial, Headstones and Markers
- State Cemetery Grants Program
- Obtaining Military Records
- Locating Veterans

VA CEMETERY WEB SITE
http://www.cem.va.gov

SPOUSE

BENEFITS FOR SPOUSE OF DECEDENT VETERAN

The surviving spouse of an honorably discharged veteran should contact the Veteran's Administration to determine whether he/she is eligible for any benefits. For example, if the decedent had minor or disabled children, his spouse may also be eligible for a monthly benefit of Dependency and Indemnity Compensation ("DIC"). If the Veteran's surviving spouse receives nursing home care under Medicaid, then the spouse might be eligible for monthly payments from the VA.

Whether a surviving spouse is eligible for any of these benefits depends on many factors including whether the decedent was serving on active duty, whether his death was service related, and the surviving spouse's assets and income. DIC benefits are discontinued should the surviving spouse remarry; however, a recent change in the law permits payments to be resumed, should the subsequent marriage end because of death or divorce.

For information about whether the surviving spouse is eligible for any benefit related to the decedent's military service call the VA at (800) 827-1000. You can receive a printed statement of public policy: VA Pamphlet 051-000-00217-2 FEDERAL BENEFITS FOR VETERANS AND DEPENDENTS by sending a check in the amount of $5 to

THE SUPERINTENDENT OF DOCUMENTS
P.O. Box 371954
Pittsburgh, PA 15250-7954

Information is also available at the VA Web site:

VA WEB SITE
http://www.va.gov

Special Situation

VICTIM COMPENSATION

If the decedent died as a result of a crime, then a family member, or anyone who lived in the same household, or who maintained a sexual relationship with the decedent, may be eligible to receive compensation for the decedent's reasonable funeral expenses (up to $5,000), psychological counseling (up to $5,000), medical expenses and loss of support. Total compensation may not exceed $45,000.

To be eligible the following must be true:

- The decedent was an innocent victim;
- The crime was reported to authorities within 48 hours of its commission or discovery of the body.
- Application for compensation was filed within 180 days from the date of death

Any of these time periods can be waived if there is some good reason for the delay.

The applicant needs to seek compensation from all other sources such as health or life insurance, or workers' compensation. Any amount received from these sources may reduce the amount awarded. (MC 27-815, 27-819, 27-820, 27-825).

You can get a Victim Compensation Claim Form by calling the Criminal Injuries Compensation Board at (410) 585-3010. Or you can download the form from the Internet:

DEPARTMENT OF PUBLIC SAFETY
AND CORRECTIONAL SERVICES
http://www.dpscs.state.md.us/

☎ LAWYER THE WRONGFUL DEATH

It is important to have a Personal Injury attorney investigate any violent or accidental death to determine whether the death was caused by the wrongful act of a person, or company. If the death was related to the decedent's job, the family may wish to consult with a Worker's Compensation attorney as well.

In Maryland, only the parent, spouse, child or a relative who was dependent on the decedent can sue for a ***wrongful death*** (i.e., one caused by a wrongful act). Only one case may be filed in name of all of the people who may be entitled to be compensated. The decedent's family has the right to be compensated for losses they suffered because of the death. The loss could be economic (loss of financial support) or non-economic (loss of companionship, mental anguish, emotional pain and suffering). In Maryland, there are limits on the amount that can be recovered for such non-economic loss. As of October, 2001 non-economic losses are limited to $605,000. That amount is scheduled to be increased each year by $15,000 (Cts. & Jud. Proc. 11-108).

The Personal Representative can file a separate suit on behalf of the decedent's estate for expenses related to the death (funeral, medical, etc.); and if the death was not instantaneous, then for the decedent's pain and suffering. There is a 3 year Statute of Limitations, so the case must be filed within 3 years from the date of death. That time can be extended if death was from an occupational disease that was not known at the time of death (Courts & Jud. Proc. 3-904).

Special Situation

THE UNCLAIMED BODY

A public officer (police, medical examiner, etc.) who has control of an unclaimed body will make a reasonable search to locate the decedent's family. If no one can be found who will take responsibility for the disposition of the body, and provided the Medical Examiner has no knowledge of any objection by the next of kin, the Medical Examiner has authority to offer the body for transplantation. If an unclaimed body is not suitable for transplantation, then any public officer may offer the body to the State Anatomy Board, for the purpose of research and study. After 48 hours has passed from the time of death, the Board may take possession of the body and transfer it to an appropriate school (Est. & Trusts 4-509, Health-Gen. 5-406).

BURYING THE INDIGENT

The state of Maryland will pay for the funeral and burial expenses of an indigent person (including inmates of a State Correctional facility), provided the decedent's family is known or registered with the Maryland Department of Human Resources. If not, and the body is unclaimed, the disposition will be as above described (Corr. Serv. 9-604, 88A-62A).

THE INDIGENT VETERAN

The federal government provides a free burial space of the honorably discharged Veteran and there may be monies available to pay for the burial and grave marker as well (see page 16).

☎ LAWYER THE MISSING BODY

Few things are more difficult to deal with than a missing person. The emotional turmoil created by the "not knowing" is often more difficult than the finality of death. The legal problems created by the disappearance are also more difficult than if the person simply died. It may take a two-part legal process — the appointment of a Guardian to handle the missing person's affairs while he is missing, and then the Probate procedure after the Court has issued an order that the missing person is dead.

APPOINTING A GUARDIAN

If a person is missing and cannot be found after a diligent search, then that person is referred to as an ***Absentee***. If the Absentee has business matters that need attending (bills that need to be paid, checks that need to be cashed, etc.), then his next of kin can ask the Probate court to appoint a Guardian of the Absentee's property and manage it, under court supervision, until the person can be found. You will need to employ an attorney, experienced in Probate matters, to get the Guardian appointed.

BEGINNING THE PROBATE PROCEDURE

Anyone who has the right to inherit the Absentee's property can begin the Probate procedure anytime that it is determined that the Absentee is dead - or -

- ⇨ Five years have passed after the appointment of a Guardian - or -
- ⇨ a year after the Absentee has been declared missing for a period of 20 years.

(Courts & Jud. Proc. 3-101, 3-102, 3-106, 3-110).

Special Situation

THE PROBLEM
FUNERAL OR BURIAL

The funeral and burial industry is well regulated by both state and federal government. Under Maryland statute (Health Occup. 7-316) the following acts are subject to disciplinary action:

- Commits fraud or misrepresentation such as delivering goods of a lesser quality that is presented to the purchaser as a sample;
- Using a false or misleading advertisement;
- Paying kick-backs to generate business;
- Providing service while under the influence of alcohol or a controlled substance;
- Discriminating in the provision of services because the decedent was HIV positive;

Funeral directors are licensed professionals so it is unusual to have a problem with the funeral or burial or cremation. However, if you had a bad experience with any aspect of the funeral then you can file a complaint with the state licensing agency:

State Board of Morticians
Department of Health and Mental Hygiene
4201 Patterson Avenue
Baltimore, MD 21215-2299
Telephone (410) 764-4792

☎ LAWYER

In addition to filing a complaint with the Board, you may wish to consult with an attorney who is experienced in litigation matters to learn of any other legal remedy that you may have.

THE DEATH CERTIFICATE

It is the job of the Funeral Director or Cremation Service Director to provide information about the decedent to the Vital Records Unit of the Maryland Department of Human Resources. The Vital Records Unit will prepare a death certificate based on that information. It is important that the information you give to the Funeral or Cremation Director is correct. It is also important that you check the form completed by the Funeral or Cremation Director to be sure names are correctly spelled and dates correctly written. Once the information is sent to Vital Records, it will be difficult and time consuming to make a correction.

The Funeral or Cremation Director will order as many certified copies of the death certificate as you request. Most establishments require an original certified copy and not a photocopy so you need to order sufficient certified copies. The following is a list of institutions that may want a certified copy:

- Each insurance company that insured the decedent or his property (health insurance, life insurance, car insurance, home insurance, etc.)
- Each financial institution in which the decedent had money invested (brokerage houses, banks)
- The decedent's pension fund
- Each credit card company used by the decedent
- The IRS and Comptroller of Maryland
- The Social Security Administration
- The Motor Vehicle Administration
- If a Probate procedure is necessary, then the Probate Court.

Some airlines and car rental companies offer a discount for short notice, emergency trips. If you have family flying in for the funeral, you may wish to order a few extra copies of the death certificate so that they can obtain an airline or car rental discount.

If you wish to order certified copies of the death certificate at a later date, you can call the funeral director and ask him to do so or you can write to:

Division of Vital Records
P.O. Box 68760
Baltimore, MD 21215-0020

You can order copies by calling (410) 764-3038. The present charge is $6 for each certified copy of the death certificate.

You can get recorded information by calling (800) 832-3277 or from the Maryland Department of Mental Hygiene Web site:

VITAL RECORDS INFORMATION
http://www.dhmh.state.md.us/

About Probate

Once a person dies, all of the property he owns as of the date of his death is referred to as the ***decedent's estate.*** If the decedent owned property that was in his name only (not jointly or in trust for someone), then some sort of court procedure is necessary to determine who is entitled to possession of the property. The name of the court procedure is ***Probate.***

In Maryland, Probate is conducted in the ***Orphan's Court***, with the exception of Harford and Montgomery counties. In those counties, the judges of the ***Circuit Court*** handle Probate matters (Est. & Trusts 2-102, 2-103). For simplicity, we will refer to the court that handles Probate matters as the ***Probate Court***, understanding that in some counties this may be the Orphan's Court and in other counties, the Circuit Court. The ***Register of Wills*** operates as the Clerk of the Court. The Register files and records the Will, collects fees, issues certified copies of documents, and generally assists people who need to file forms with the Probate Court (Est. & Trusts 2-206, 2-208).

The root of the word Probate is "to prove." It refers to the first job of the Probate Court, that is, to examine proof of whether the decedent left a valid Will or whether he died ***intestate*** (without a Will). The second job of the Probate Court is to appoint someone to wrap up the affairs of the decedent — to pay any outstanding bills and then to distribute what property is left to the beneficiaries.

If the decedent died without a Will, then the Probate Court will appoint someone to be the ***Administrator*** of the estate and issue ***Letters of Administration.*** If the decedent left a valid Will naming someone as ***Executor*** of his estate, then the Probate Court will appoint that person for the job. For simplicity we will refer to the person appointed by the court to administer the decedent's estate as the ***Personal Representative***, and the document authorizing him to act, as ***Letters*** (Est. & Trusts 1-101).

There are different ways to conduct a Probate procedure depending on the value of the property that is being Probated. We will refer to property that is distributed as part of a Probate procedure as the decedent's ***Probate Estate*** and the method of conducting a Probate procedure as the ***Estate Administration***. Chapter 6 explains the different kinds of estate administration that are available in Maryland.

But we are getting ahead of ourselves. First we need to determine whether a Probate procedure is necessary. To answer that question we need to know exactly what the decedent owned, so the next two chapters explain how to identify, and then locate, all of the decedent's assets.

Giving Notice Of The Death 2

Those closest to the decedent usually notify family members and close friends by telephone. The funeral director will arrange to have an obituary published in as many different newspapers as the family requests, but there is still the job of notifying the government and people who were doing business with the decedent. That job is the duty of whoever is appointed as Personal Representative of the decedent's estate.

Maryland law gives an order of priority for the appointment of Personal Representative. Whoever the decedent named as Personal Representative in his Will has top priority. If that person is unable or unwilling to serve, then the surviving spouse is next in line. If there is no surviving spouse, or the spouse is unable or unwilling to serve, then the job falls to the ***residuary beneficiaries*** i.e., whoever stands to inherit the decedent's property once all special gifts are distributed and bills paid (Est. & Trusts 5-104).

If there is no Will, the decedent's spouse and children have an equal right to be appointed as Personal Representative, so it is their job to give notice of the death. If there is no spouse or child, the job falls to his next of kin. By ***next of kin,*** we mean those people who inherit the decedent's property according to Maryland's LAWS OF INTESTATE SUCCESSION. Those laws are explained in Chapter 5.

NOTIFYING SOCIAL SECURITY

Many Funeral Directors will, as part of their service package, notify the Social Security Administration of the death. You may wish to check to see that this has been done. You can do so by calling (800) 772-1213. If you are hearing impaired call (800) 325-0778 TTY. You will need to give the Social Security Administration the full legal name of the decedent as well as his social security number and date of birth.

Special Situation

DECEDENT RECEIVING SOCIAL SECURITY CHECKS

If the decedent was receiving checks from Social Security, then you need to determine whether his last check needs to be returned to the Social Security Administration.

Each Social Security check is a payment for the prior month, provided that person lives for the entire prior month. If someone dies on the last day of the month, then you should not cash the check for that month. For example, if someone dies on July 31st, then you need to return the check that the agency mails out in August. If however, the decedent died on August 1st then the check sent in August need not be returned because that check is payment for the month of July.

If the Social Security check is electronically deposited into a bank account, then notify the bank that the account holder died and notify the Social Security Administration as well. If the check needs to be returned, then the Social Security Administration will withdraw it electronically from the bank account. You will need to keep the account open until the funds are withdrawn.

SPOUSE

SPOUSE/CHILD'S SOCIAL SECURITY BENEFITS

If the decedent had sufficient work credits, the Social Security Administration will give the decedent's widow(er) or if unmarried, then the decedent's minor children, a one-time death benefit of $255.

SURVIVORS BENEFITS:

The spouse (or ex-spouse) of the decedent may be eligible for Survivors Benefits. Benefits vary depending on the amount of work credits earned by the decedent; whether the decedent had minor or disabled children; the spouse's age; how long they were married; etc. The minor child of the decedent may be eligible for benefits regardless of whether the child's father (the decedent) ever married the child's mother. Paternity can be established by any one of several methods including the father acknowledging his child in writing or verbally to members of his family. For more information you can call the Social Security Administration at (800) 772-1213.

SOCIAL SECURITY BENEFITS

A spouse or ex-spouse can collect social security benefits based on the decedent's work record. This value may be greater than the spouse now receives. It is important to make an appointment with your local Social Security office and determine whether you as the spouse (or ex-spouse) or parent of decedent's minor child are eligible for any Social Security or Survivor benefit. The Social Security Administration has a Web site from which you can down load publications that explain survivors benefits:

SOCIAL SECURITY WEB SITE
http://www.ssa.gov

Special Situation

DECEDENT WITH GOVERNMENT PENSION

Any pension or annuity check received after the date of death of a federal retiree, or a survivor annuitant, needs to be returned to the U.S. Treasury. If the check is direct deposited to a bank account, then call the financial institution and ask them to return the check. If the check is sent by mail then you need to return it to:

Director, Regional Finance Center
U. S. Treasury Department
P.O. Box 7367
Chicago, IL 60680

Include a letter explaining the reason for the return of the check and stating the decedent's date of death.

$$$ APPLY FOR BENEFITS $$$

A survivor annuity may be available to a surviving spouse, and/or minor or disabled child. In some cases, a former spouse may be eligible for benefits. Even though you notify the government of the death, they will not automatically give you benefits to which you may be entitled. You need to apply for those benefits by notifying the Office of Personnel Management ("OPM") of the death and requesting that they send you an application for survivor benefits. You can call them at (888) 767-6738 or you can write to:

THE OFFICE OF PERSONNEL MANAGEMENT
SERVICE AND RECORDS CENTER
BOYERS, PA 16017

You will find brochures and information about Survivor's Benefits at the OPM Web site:

OFFICE OF PERSONNEL MANAGEMENT WEB SITE
http://www.opm.gov

Special Situation

DECEDENT WITH COMPANY PENSION OR ANNUITY

In most cases, pension and annuity checks are payment for the prior month. If the decedent received his pension or annuity check before his death, then no monies need be returned. Pension checks and/or annuity checks received after the date of death may need to be returned to the company. You need to notify the company of the death to determine the status of the last check sent to the decedent.

Before notifying the company, locate the policy or pension statement that is the basis of the income. That document should tell whether there is a beneficiary of the pension or annuity funds now that the pensioner or annuitant is dead. If you cannot locate the document, use the return address on the check envelope and ask the company to send you a copy of the plan. Also request that they forward to you any claim form that may be required in order for the survivor or beneficiary to receive benefits under that pension plan or policy.

If the pension/annuity check is direct deposited to the decedent's account, then ask the bank to assist you in locating the company and notifying the company of the death.

Special Situation

DECEDENT WITH AN IRA or a QUALIFIED RETIREMENT PLAN ("QRP")

Anyone who is a beneficiary of an Individual Retirement Account ("IRA") or QRP needs to keep in mind that no income taxes have been paid on monies placed in an IRA or QRP account. Once monies are withdrawn, significant taxes may be due. You need to learn what options are available to you as a beneficiary of the plan and the tax consequences of each option. You will need to ask an accountant how much will be due in taxes for each option. Once you know all the facts, you will be able to make the best choice for your circumstance.

SPOUSE

If the spouse is the beneficiary of the decedent's IRA account, then there are special options available. The spouse has the right to withdraw the money from the account or roll it over into the spouse's own retirement account. Although the employer can explain options that are available, the spouse still needs to understand the tax consequence of choosing any given option. It is important to consult with an accountant to determine the best way to go.

If the decedent had a QRP, the plan may permit the spouse to roll the balance of the account into a new IRA. The spouse needs to contact the decedent's employer for an explanation of the plan and all the options that are available at this time.

NOTIFYING IRS

THE FINAL INCOME TAX RETURN

The decedent's final income tax return (IRS form 1040) needs to be filed by April 15th of the year following the year in which he died. The state income tax is filed at the same time (Tax Gen 10-813). If the decedent was married, then the surviving spouse can file a final joint return. If there is no surviving spouse, then it is the Personal Representative's job to file the final income tax returns.

If no Probate procedure is necessary, then whoever inherits the decedent's property needs to file the final income tax returns. If you have a joint bank account with the decedent, do not close that account until you determine whether the decedent is entitled to an income tax refund. See Chapter 6 for an explanation of how to obtain a refund from the IRS.

THE GOOD NEWS

Monies inherited from the decedent are generally not counted as income to you, so you do not pay federal income tax on those monies. If the monies you inherit later earn interest or income for you, then of course you will report that income as you do any other type of income.

Special Situation

BENEFICIARY OF A MARYLAND HOMESTEAD

In Maryland, homeowners' tax exemptions are allowed for any number of reasons such as the owner being blind, or a disabled veteran, or the surviving spouse of a blind person or a disabled veteran. In addition to homeowners' tax exemptions there is a Homestead Property Tax Credit for those who are over 60, or disabled, or of low income, or living with dependent children (Tax-Property 7-207, 7-208, 9-102, 9-104).

If the decedent was receiving a tax exemption or credit, then the Maryland Department of Assessments and Taxation must be notified of the change of ownership. If you have inherited Maryland property that you intend to occupy as your principal residence, you may be eligible for your own homestead tax exemption or credit. You can get information about how to apply for these benefits from the Maryland Department of Assessments and Taxation at (800) 944-7403. You can get Tax Credit and Exemption information and download forms from their Web site:

MARYLAND DEPT. OF ASSESSMENTS AND TAXATION
http://www.dat.state.md.us/

SPOUSE SELLING THE HOME

In the tough "ole days" the IRS used to allow capital gains tax exclusion (up to $125,000) on the sale of one's homestead (the principal residence). A person had to be 55 or older to take advantage of the exclusion, and it was a once-in-a-lifetime tax break. If a married couple sold their home and took the exclusion it was "used up" and no longer available to either partner.

In these, the good times, the IRS allows you to sell your homestead and up to $250,000 ($500,000 for a married couple) of the home-sale profit is tax free (IRC Section 121 (b) 3). There is no limit on the number of times you can use the exclusion, provided you own and live in the homestead at least two years prior to the sale.

If the decedent and his spouse used their "once in a lifetime" homestead tax exclusion, with this new law, the surviving spouse can sell the homestead and once again take advantage of a tax break.

TAX BREAKS FOR SURVIVING SPOUSE

In Maryland, homeowners' tax exemptions are available for disabled veterans and for blind persons. Tax credits are available for the aged, disabled and those with low income. If the decedent was receiving such exemption or credit, and the surviving spouse is now the owner of that homestead, then the spouse may be entitled to the same exemption for so long as the surviving spouse remains unmarried. The spouse will need to apply to the local Assessment Office for the exemption or credit (Tax-Property 7-207, 7-208, 9-104).

THE MARYLAND INHERITANCE TAX

Maryland imposes an Inheritance Tax on property transferred as a result of the decedent's death. This includes property that passes by Will or Trust or according to Maryland's Laws of Intestate Succession, joint property, etc. It also includes property that the decedent transferred at any time two years before he died, provided the transfer was made because the decedent knew he was dying. It does not include life insurance benefits paid to anyone other than the estate of the decedent. It does not include payments received under an employees' pension or benefit plan, provided those payments are not taxable for Federal Estate Tax purposes (Tax-Gen. 7-201, 7-203).

The current rate for the Inheritance Tax is 10% of the "clear value" which is defined to be the market value, less any expense related to the transfer. The Register of Wills determines the actual value that must be paid. If no Probate procedure is necessary, then an Information Report must still be filed with the Register. Whoever is entitled to receive the property must pay the taxes due on that property (Tax-Gen 7-214, 7-231, 7-308).

NO TAX FOR IMMEDIATE FAMILY

No Inheritance Tax need be paid for property that is transferred to the decedent's spouse or the decedent's ***descendant*** (child, grandchild, great-grandchild, etc.) or the spouse of a descendent, or the decedent's parent, grandparent, stepparent, stepchild, brother or sister. There is no tax for transfers of $1,000 or less. For more information call the office of the Comptroller of Maryland at (800) 638-2927. Out of state call (410) 260-7850. You can also get information from the Comptrollers Web site:

COMPTROLLER OF MARYLAND
http://individuals.marylandtaxes.com

AN ESTATE TAX FOR THE WEALTHY

The ***Taxable Estate*** of the decedent is the total value of all of his property, as of his date of death. This includes real property (homestead, vacant lots, etc.) and personal property (cars, life insurance policies, business interests, securities, IRA accounts, etc.). It includes property held in the decedent's name alone, as well as property that he held jointly or in trust for another.

An ***Estate Tax*** is a tax imposed by the federal and state government for the transfer of property at death. There is a federal ***Gift Tax*** on gifts given during a person's lifetime that exceed $10,000 per person, per year. Should a gift be given that exceeds $10,000, that gift must be reported to the IRS, but no tax need be paid unless the total value of gifts made in excess of $10,000 previously made by that person, exceeds a certain amount as set by the government. Once a person dies the cumulative value of gifts reported to IRS in excess of $10,000 per year is added to the decedent's Taxable Estate. No federal Estate Tax need be paid unless the combined sum exceed the exemption amount as set by the federal government. This amount is scheduled to increase as follows:

YEAR	EXEMPTION AMOUNT
2002-2003	$1,000,000
2004-2005	$1,500,000
2006-2008	$2,000,000
2009	$3,500,000

The Maryland Estate tax is equal to the maximum state death tax credit that is allowed on the federal return, less any inheritance tax paid to the Register of Wills (Tax-Gen 7-304). There is an unlimited marital tax deduction for property transferred to the surviving spouse; so in most cases, no tax need be paid if the decedent was married; however, an Estate Tax return must be filed whenever the decedent's estate exceeds the exemption amount in effect as of his date of death.

The current federal Estate Tax is scheduled to be phased out in the year 2010, but a new Capital Gains Tax is scheduled for 2010 that may prove even more costly than the Estate Tax. The new Capital Gains Tax is related to the way inherited property is evaluated by the federal government. Real and personal property is inherited at a "step up" in basis. This means that if the decedent purchased an item that is worth more than when he purchased it, the beneficiary will inherit the property at its fair market value as of the decedent's date of death. For example, if the decedent bought stock for $20,000 and it is worth $50,000 as of the date of death, his beneficiary will take a step-up in basis of $30,000, meaning that the beneficiary inherits the stock at the $50,000 value. If the beneficiary sells the stock for $50,000, he pays no Capital Gains tax. If the beneficiary holds onto the stock and later sells it for $60,000, the beneficiary will pay a Capital Gains tax only on the $10,000 increase in value since the decedent's death.

Up to 2009, there is no limit to the amount you can take as a step-up in basis. But in 2010 caps are set in place. The decedent's estate will be allowed a 1.3 million dollar set up in basis, plus another 3 million for property passing to the surviving spouse. The new law could result in significant Capital Gains taxes that the beneficiary must pay. For example, suppose in 2010 you inherit a business from your father that he purchased for $100,000 and it is now worth 2 million dollars. There is a capital gain of 1.9 million dollars, but you are allowed a step-up in basis of only 1.3 million; so $600,000 of your inheritance is subject to a Capital Gains tax.

No one knows how the new law will be applied in 2010, but it could well be that the Capital Gains tax on your inheritance turns out to be the same as, if not more than, what you would have paid in Estate Taxes, before they were "phased out."

THE UN-UNIFIED GIFT TAX

As explained on page 37, the Gift Tax is unified with the Estate Tax so that if you give a gift to someone in excess of $10,000, the amount over $10,000 is added to your Taxable Estate. Up until the change in the law, you did not need to pay a Gift Tax during your lifetime unless the amount given during your lifetime exceeded the tax credit. That changes in 2004. In 2004, the Estate Tax credit goes up to $1,500,000, but the Gift Tax credit remains at $1,000,000 so they are no longer unified.

Specifically, if you make a gift to anyone of more than $10,000 per year, the amount over $10,000 must be reported to the IRS. The IRS keeps a running count of the reported values. As of 2004, once the sum of all of your reported values exceed $1,000,000, you will pay a Gift Tax on any amount that you give during your lifetime that exceeds $10,000 per person per year.

The Estate Tax is scheduled to be repealed in 2010, but not the Gift Tax.

Special Situation DECEDENT WITH A TRUST

If the decedent was the Grantor (or Settlor) of a Trust, then he was probably managing the Trust as Trustee during his lifetime. The Trust document should name a ***Successor Trustee*** to manage the Trust now that the Grantor is deceased. The Trust document may instruct the Successor Trustee to make certain gifts once the Grantor dies or the Trust document may direct the Successor Trustee to hold money in Trust for a beneficiary of the Trust.

☎ **LAWYER** IF YOU ARE SUCCESSOR TRUSTEE

If you are the Successor Trustee then in addition to following the terms of the Trust, you are required to obey all of the laws of the state of Maryland relating to the administration of the Trust. You should consult with an attorney experienced in Estate Planning to help you administer the Trust according to the law and without any liability to yourself .

IF YOU ARE A BENEFICIARY

If you are a beneficiary of the Trust, then you need to obtain a copy of the Trust provisions that apply to you and learn how the Trust will be administered now that the Grantor or Settlor is deceased. Most Trust documents are written in "legalese," so you may want to employ your own attorney to review the Trust, and explain your rights under that Trust.

NOTIFYING THE BUSINESS COMMUNITY

People and companies who were doing business with the decedent need to be notified of his death. This includes utility companies, banks, brokerage firms and any company that insured the decedent.

NOTIFY INSURANCE COMPANIES

Examine the decedent's financial records to determine the name and telephone number of all of the companies that insured the decedent or his property. This includes real property insurance, motor vehicle insurance, health insurance and life insurance.

MOTOR VEHICLE INSURANCE

Locate the insurance policy for all motor vehicles owed by the decedent (car, truck, boat, airplane) and notify the insurance company of the death. Determine how long insurance coverage continues after the death. Ask the insurance agent to explain what things are covered under the policy. Is the motor vehicle covered for all types of casualty (theft, accident, vandalism, etc.) or is coverage limited in some way?

If you can continue coverage, then determine when the next insurance payment is due. Hopefully, the car will be sold or transferred to a beneficiary before that date, but if not, you need to arrange for sufficient insurance coverage during the Probate procedure.

LIFE INSURANCE COMPANIES

You need to determine whether the decedent had life insurance, and if so, then you need to locate the policy and notify the company of his death. Call each life insurance company and ask what they require in order to forward the insurance proceeds to the beneficiary. Most companies will want the original policy and a certified copy of the death certificate.

Send the original policy by certified mail or any of the overnight services that require a signed receipt for the package. Make a copy of the original policy for your records before mailing the original policy to the company.

IF YOU CANNOT LOCATE THE POLICY

If you know that the decedent was insured, but you cannot locate the insurance policy, you can contact the company and request a copy of the policy. A tougher question is how to locate the policy if you can't find the policy and do not know the name of the insurance company. The American Council of Life Insurers offers suggestions that you may find helpful at the Missing Policy Inquiry page of their Web site:

AMERICAN COUNCIL OF LIFE INSURERS WEB SITE
http://www.acli.com

IF YOU CANNOT LOCATE THE COMPANY

If you cannot locate the insurance company it may be doing business under another name or it may no longer be doing business in the state of Maryland. Each state has a branch of government that regulates insurance companies doing business in that state. If you are having difficulty locating the insurance company call the Department of Insurance in the state where the policy was purchased and ask for assistance in locating the company. In Maryland call the Maryland Insurance Administration at (800) 492-6116. For the hearing impaired call (800) 725-2258 (TTY).

EAGLE PUBLISHING COMPANY OF BOCA has the telephone number for the Department of Insurance for each state at their Web site:

EAGLE PUBLISHING COMPANY OF BOCA WEB SITE
http://www.eaglepublishing.com

Special Situation ACCIDENTAL DEATH

If the decedent died as a result of an accident, then check for all possible sources of accident insurance coverage including his homeowner's policy. Some credit card companies provide accident insurance as part of their contract with their card holders.

If the decedent died in an automobile accident, check to see whether he was covered by any type of travel insurance, such as rental car insurance. If he belonged to an automobile club, such as AAA, then check whether he had accident insurance as part of his club membership.

HOMEOWNER'S INSURANCE

If the decedent owned his own home, then check whether there is sufficient insurance coverage on the property. The decedent may have neglected to increase his insurance as the property appreciated in value. If you think the property may be vacant for some period of time, then it is important to have vandalism coverage included in the policy. Once the property is sold, or transferred to the proper beneficiary, you can have the policy discontinued or transferred to the new owner. The decedent's estate should receive a rebate for the unused portion of the premium.

MORTGAGE INSURANCE

If the decedent had a mortgage on any parcel of real estate that he owned, he might have arranged with his lender for an insurance policy that pays off the mortgage balance in the event of his death. Look at the closing statement to see if there was a charge for mortgage insurance. Also check with the lender to determine if such a policy was purchased.

If the decedent was the sole owner of the property, and no provision was made to pay off the loan, then the beneficiary of that property needs to contact the lender and arrange to either pay off the loan or to assume liability for the mortgage.

NOTIFY THE HOMEOWNER'S ASSOCIATION

If the decedent owned a condominium or a residence regulated by a homeowner's association, then the association will need to be notified of the death. Once the property is transferred to the proper beneficiary, he/she will need to contact the association to learn the rules and regulations regarding ownership and to arrange to have notices of dues and assessments forwarded to the new owner.

WORK RELATED INSURANCE

If the decedent was employed, then check his records for information about work related benefits. He may have survivor benefits from a company or group life insurance plan and/or a retirement plan. Also check with the employer about company benefits. If the decedent belonged to a union, then contact them to determine whether there are any union benefits.

The decedent may have belonged to a professional, fraternal or social organization such as the local Chamber of Commerce, a Veteran's organization, the Kiwanis, AARP, the Rotary Club, etc. If he belonged to any such organization check to see whether the organization provided any type of insurance coverage.

Special Situation **BUSINESS OWNED BY DECEDENT**

If the decedent owned his own company or was a partner in a company he may have purchased "key man" insurance. Key man insurance is a policy designed to protect the company should a valuable employee become disabled or die. Benefits are paid to the company to compensate the company for the loss of someone who is essential to the continuation of the business. Ultimately the policy benefits those who inherit the business.

If the decedent had an ownership interest in an ongoing business (sole proprietor, shareholder or partner) there may be a shareholder's or partnership agreement requiring the company to purchase the decedent's share of the business. The Personal Representative's attorney needs to investigate to see if there was a key man insurance policy and/or such purchase agreement.

Special Situation

CORPORATE OWNER OR RESIDENT AGENT

If the decedent was the sole owner of a corporation and the company stock was in his name only, then there may need to be a Probate procedure in order to transfer the company to the new owner.

Maryland law requires each corporation to continuously maintain a Resident Agent who resides in this state. If the decedent was the sole officer and/or Resident Agent of the company then the Maryland State Department of Assessments and Taxation needs to be notified of the identity of the new officers and/or Resident Agent as soon as is practicable (Corp. 2-108).

Forms to provide notice of the change of officers, directors and Resident Agent can be obtained by calling (410) 767-1184 or by writing to them at:

State Department of Assessments and Taxation
301 W. Preston Street
Baltimore, MD 21201

If you were not actively involved in running the business, then you might request a status report of the company. The report will show whether filing fees are current and will identify the officers and Resident Agent of the company. The Department of Assessments and Taxation has a Web site from which you can obtain information about Maryland corporations:

STATE DEPT. OF ASSESSMENTS AND TAXATION
http://www.dat.state.md.us/

NOTIFY ADVERTISERS

Probably the last in the world to learn of the decedent's death is the direct mail advertiser. Advertisers are nothing if not tenacious. It is not uncommon for advertisements to be mailed to the decedent for more than ten years after the death. It is not because the advertiser is trying to sell something to the decedent, but rather the people who prepare (and sell) mailing lists do not know that the person is dead.

Those who sell mailing lists may not be motivated to update the list because of the cost of doing the necessary research; and maybe even because the price of the mailing list is often based on the number of people on the list. Even those who compose their own list may decide it is less costly to mail to everyone, than take the time (and money) to update the list.

If it gives you pleasure to think of advertisers spending substantial sums for nothing, then that is what you should do (nothing). But for those of you who wince each time you see another piece of mail addressed to the decedent, you can write to the Direct Marketing Association and ask that the name be deleted from all mailing lists:

Mail Preference Service
Direct Marketing Association
P.O. Box 9008
Farmingdale, NY 11735

You will need to give them the decedent's complete address, including zip code and every name variation that the decedent may have used; for example:

Mr. Theodore James Jones
Ted Jones　　Ted J. Jones
T. J. Jones　　T. James Jones, etc.

HEALTH INSURANCE

The Health Insurance carrier probably knows of the death, but it is a good idea to contact them to determine what coverage the decedent had under that insurance plan. If you cannot find the original policy, have the insurance company send you a copy of the policy so that you can determine whether medical treatment given to the decedent before his death was covered by that policy.

Special Situation

DECEDENT ON MEDICARE

If the decedent was covered by Medicare, you do not need to notify anyone, but you do need to know what things were covered by Medicare so that you can determine what medical bills are (or are not) covered by Medicare. The publication MEDICARE AND YOU explains what things are covered. The book is available in regular print (Publication HCFA 10050) and in large print (Publication HCFA 10050-LE). You can get the book by writing to the

U.S. GOVERNMENT PRINTING OFFICE
U.S. Dept. of Health and Human Services
Health Care Financing Administration
7500 Security Boulevard
Baltimore, MD 21244-1850

You can also find the publication on the Internet:

MEDICARE WEB SITE
http:/www.medicare.gov

SPOUSE

THE SPOUSE'S HEALTH INSURANCE

If the spouse of the decedent is insured under Medicare, then the death does not affect the surviving spouse's coverage. If spouse was not covered by Medicare but has her own health insurance that also covered the decedent, then the spouse needs to notify the employer of the death because this may affect the cost of the plan to the employer and/or the spouse.

If the spouse was covered under the decedent's policy then he/she needs to arrange for new coverage. There are state and federal laws that ensure continued coverage under the decedent's policy for a period of time depending on whether the decedent's employer falls under federal or state regulation.

If the decedent was employed by a federally regulated company (usually a company with at least twenty employees) then under the Consolidated Omnibus Budget Reconciliation Act ("COBRA") the employer must make the company health plan available to the surviving spouse and any dependent child of the decedent for at least 36 months. The employer is required to give notice to the surviving spouse that the spouse and/or dependent child have the right to continue coverage under the decedent's health plan.

The spouse and/or child have 60 days from the date of death or 60 days after the employer sends notice (whichever is later) to tell the employer whether the surviving spouse and child wish to continue with the health insurance plan (29 USC 18 Sec. 1162, 1163).

SPOUSE'S HEALTH INSURANCE (continued)

The only problem with continued coverage may be the cost. Before the death, the employer may have been paying some percentage of the premium. The employer has no such duty after the death unless there was some employment agreement stating otherwise. Under COBRA, the employer may charge the spouse for the full cost of the plan plus a 2% administrative fee.

If you have a question about your coverage under COBRA, you can call the U.S. Department of Labor ("DOL") at (800) 998-7542 and ask for the number of your local DOL office. You can also ask that they send you their publication HEALTH BENEFITS UNDER COBRA; or you can visit their Web site for more information:

DEPARTMENT OF LABOR WEB SITE
http://www.dol.gov/dol/pwba

CONTINUED COVERAGE UNDER MARYLAND LAW

Employers who cover 100 employees or less under a group health insurance policy, must offer the surviving spouse and/or dependent children continued coverage under that policy for at least 18 months following the death. To be eligible for continued coverage, the decedent must have been employed by that employer for at least 3 months before the death; and the spouse and/or child must notify the employer that they wish to continue coverage within 45 days of the date of death. Coverage must be the same as before the death. The cost must be the same as paid by the decedent, however, as with Cobra, the employer is entitled to a reasonable administrative fee (Insur. 15-407, 15-415).

✍ CHANGE BENEFICIARIES ✍

If the decedent was someone you named as beneficiary of your insurance policy, Will or Trust, brokerage account or pension plan, then you may need to name another beneficiary in his place:

INSURANCE POLICY ✍

If you named the decedent as the primary beneficiary of your life insurance policy, then check to see whether you named a contingent (alternate) beneficiary in the event that the decedent did not survive you. If not, then you need to contact the insurance company and name a new beneficiary. If you did name a contingent beneficiary, then that person is now your primary beneficiary and you need to consider whether you wish to name a new contingent beneficiary at this time.

HEALTH INSURANCE POLICY ✍

If the decedent was covered under your health insurance policy, then your employer and the health insurer need to be notified of the death because this may affect the cost of the plan to you and/or your employer.

WILL OR TRUST ✍

Most Wills provide for a contingent beneficiary in the event that the person named as beneficiary dies first. If you named the decedent as your beneficiary, then check to see whether you named an alternate beneficiary. If not, you need to have your attorney revise your Will and name a new beneficiary.

Similarly, if you are the Grantor or Settlor of a Trust and the decedent was one of the beneficiaries of your Trust, then check the Trust document to see if you named an alternate beneficiary. If not, contact your attorney to prepare an amendment to the Trust, naming a new beneficiary.

BANK AND SECURITIES ACCOUNTS ✍

If the decedent was a beneficiary of your bank or securities account, or if the decedent was a joint owner of your bank account or securities account, then it is important to contact the financial institution and tell them about the death. You may wish to arrange for a new beneficiary or joint owner at this time.

PENSION PLANS ✍

If the decedent was a beneficiary under your pension plan, then you need to notify them of his death and name a new beneficiary. Many pension plans require that you notify them within a set period of time (usually 30 days) so it is important to notify them as soon as you are able. If the decedent was a beneficiary of your Individual Retirement Account ("IRA") or of your Qualified Retirement Plan ("QRP") and you did not provide for an alternate beneficiary, then you need to name someone at this time.

Before you choose an alternate beneficiary, it is important that you understand all of the options available to you. Not an easy task. There are many complex government regulations relating to IRA and QRP accounts. And even if you believe you understood your options when you set up your account, they are scheduled to be changed beginning in 2002. You can read about the proposed regulations under 42 U.S.C 401(a)(9) in the *Federal Register* that was published on January 17, 2001, but unless you have an extensive tax background, it is just so much "legalese," i.e., incomprehensible without a professional to translate it into plain English.

Your choice of beneficiary can impact the amount of money you can withdraw each month, so it is important to consult with your accountant or tax attorney or financial planner, before you make your election.

NOTIFY CREDIT CARD COMPANIES

You need to notify the decedent's credit card companies of the death. If you can find the contract with the credit card company check to see whether the decedent had credit card insurance. If the decedent had credit card insurance, then the balance of the account is now paid in full. If you cannot find the contract contact the company and get a copy of the contract along with a statement of the balance due as of the date of death.

DESTROY DECEDENT'S CREDIT CARDS

You need to destroy all of the decedent's credit cards. If you hold a credit card jointly with the decedent, then it is important to waste no time in closing that account and opening another in your name only.

That's something Barbara knows from hard experience. She and Hank never married but they did live together for several years before he died from liver disease. Hank came from a well to do family so he had enough money to support himself and Barbara during his long illness. Hank put Barbara on all of his credit card accounts so that she could purchase things when he became too ill to go shopping with her. After the funeral, Barbara had a gathering of friends and family at their apartment. Barbara was so preoccupied with her loss that she never noticed that Hank's credit cards were missing until the bills started coming in.

Barbara did not know who ran up the bills on Hank's credit cards during the month following his death. It was obvious that Hank's signature had been forged — but who forged it? One credit card company suspected that it might have been Barbara herself. Because the cards were held jointly, Barbara became liable to either pay the debts or prove that she did not make the purchases. She was able to clear her credit record but it took several months and she had to employ an attorney to do so.

NOTIFYING OTHER CREDITORS

If a Probate procedure is necessary and the decedent owed money, then it is the job of the person appointed as Personal Representative to notify the decedent's creditors of the death. The attorney who handles the Probate will explain to the Personal Representative how notice is to be given.

If no Probate procedure is necessary, then the next of kin can notify the creditors of the death, but before doing so, read Chapter 4: WHAT BILLS NEED TO BE PAID? That chapter explains what bills need to be paid and who is responsible to pay them.

Before any bill can be paid you need to know whether the decedent left any assets that could be used to pay those debts. The next chapter explains how to identify, and then locate all of the property owned by the decedent.

Locating the Assets 3

It is important to locate the financial records of the decedent and then carefully examine those records. Even the partner of a long-term marriage should conduct a thorough search because the surviving spouse may be unaware of all that was owned (or owed) by the decedent.

It is not unusual for a surviving spouse to be surprised when learning of the decedent's business transactions, especially in those cases where the decedent had control of family finances. One such example is that of Sam and Henrietta. They married just as soon as Sam was discharged from the army after World War II. During their marriage, Sam handled all of the finances giving Henrietta just enough money to run the household.

Every now and again Henrietta would think of getting a job. She longed to have her own source of income and some economic independence. Each time she brought up the subject Sam would loudly object. He had no patience for this new "woman's lib" thing. Sam said he got married to have a real wife — one who would cook his meals and keep house for him.

Henrietta was not the arguing type. She rationalized, saying that Sam had a delicate stomach and dust allergies. He needed her to prepare his special meals and keep an immaculate house for him. Besides, Sam had a good job with a major cruise line and he needed her to accompany him on his frequent business trips.

Once Sam retired, he was even more cautious in his spending habits. Henrietta seldom complained. She assumed the reason for his "thrift" was that they had little money and had to live on his pension.

They were married 52 years when Sam died at the age of 83. Henrietta was 81 at the time of his death. She was one very happy, very angry and very aged widow when she discovered that Sam left her with assets worth well over a million dollars!

LOCATING RECORDS

As you go through the papers of the decedent you may come across documents that indicate property ownership, such as bank registers, stock or bond certificates, insurance policies, brokerage account statements, etc. Place all evidence of ownership in a single place. You will need to contact the different companies in order to transfer title to the proper beneficiary. Chapter 5 explains how to identify the proper beneficiary of the decedent's property. Chapter 6 explains how to transfer the property to that beneficiary.

You may also need to produce evidence of the decedent's personal relationships, such as a marriage certificate, birth certificate, or naturalization papers, a Final Judgement of Divorce, military personnel records, etc. If you cannot locate his marriage certificate or birth certificate, you can get a certified copy of those records from the Vital Records office in the state where the event took place. See page 24 for Maryland's Vital Records. You can find the location and telephone number for other states by calling information or from the Internet by using your favorite search engine to locate Vital Records.

For deceased veterans, you can obtain a copy of his military record by writing to:

The National Personnel Records Center
Military Personnel Records
9700 Page Avenue
St. Louis, MO 63132-5100

They will send you form SF 180 to complete. You can get the form from the Internet at http://www.cem.va.gov or from the National Archives and Records Administration Fax-On-Demand system. Dial (301) 713-6905 and request document number 2255.

COLLECT AND IDENTIFY KEYS

The decedent may have kept his records in a safe deposit box, so you may find that your first job is to locate the keys to the box. As you go through the personal effects of the decedent, collect and identify all the keys that you find. If you come across an unidentified key, it could be a key to a post office box (private or federal) or a safe deposit box located in a bank or in a private vault company. You will need to determine whether that key opens a box that contains property belonging to the decedent or whether the key is to a box no longer in use. Some ways to investigate are as follows:

☑ CHECK BUSINESS RECORDS

If the decedent kept receipts, look through those items to see if he paid for the rental of a post office or safe deposit box. Also, look at his check register to see if he wrote a check to the Postmaster or to any safe deposit or vault company. Look at his bank statements to see if there is any bank charge for a safe deposit box. Some banks bill separately for safe deposit boxes so check with all of the banks in which the decedent had an account to determine if he had a safe deposit box with that bank.

☑ CHECK THE KEY TYPE

If you cannot identify the key, then take it to each local locksmith and ask whether anyone can identify the type of facility that uses such keys. If that doesn't work, go to each bank, post office and private safe deposit boxes located in places where the decedent shopped, worked or frequented and ask whether they use the type of key that you found.

☑ CHECK THE MAIL

Check the mail over the next several months to see if the decedent receives a statement requesting payment for the next year's rental of a post office or safe deposit box.

FORWARD THE DECEDENT'S MAIL

You may find evidence of a brokerage account, bank account, or safe deposit box by examining correspondence addressed to the decedent. If the decedent was living alone, then have the mail forwarded to the person he named as Personal Representative or Executor of his Will. If the decedent did not leave a Will then the mail should be forwarded to his next of kin. Call the Postmaster and ask him/her to send you the necessary forms to make the change. Request that the mail be forwarded for the longest period allowed by law (currently one year).

The decedent may have been renting a post office box at his local post office branch or perhaps at the branch closest to where he did his banking. Ask the Postmaster to help you determine whether the decedent was renting a post office box. If so, then you need to locate the key to the box so that you can collect the decedent's mail.

Special Situation

LOST POST OFFICE BOX KEY

If the decedent had a post office box and you cannot locate the key, then contact the local postmaster and ask him/her what documentation is needed for you to gain possession of the mail in that box. As before, you will ask the Postmaster to have all future mail addressed to that box, forwarded to the Personal Representative, or if there is no Will, then to the decedent's next of kin.

WHAT TO DO WITH CHECKS

You may receive checks in the mail made out to the decedent. Social security checks, pension checks and annuity checks issued after the date of death may need to be returned to the sender. (See pages 28 and 30 of this book.) Other checks need to be deposited. If a Probate procedure is necessary, then the Personal Representative will open a Probate Estate account and will deposit the decedent's checks to that account.

If no Probate procedure is necessary, then checks can be deposited to any account held in the name of the decedent. The decedent is not here to endorse the check, but you can deposit to his account by writing his bank account number on the back of the check and printing beneath it "FOR DEPOSIT ONLY."

The bank will accept such an endorsement and deposit the check into the decedent's account. If the check is significant in value and/or the decedent had different accounts that are accessible to different people, then there needs to be cooperation and a sense of fair play. If not, the dollar gain may not nearly offset the emotional turmoil.

Such was the case with Gail. Her father made her a joint owner of his checking account to assist in paying his bills. He had macular degeneration and it was increasingly difficult for him to see. The father also had a savings account that was in his name only that he held in trust for his two children; i.e., he gave the bank instructions that upon his death the money was to be divided equally between Gail and Ken.

Ken had a good paying job in Alaska. Even though he lived at a distance, Ken, his wife and two children always spent the Christmas holidays with his father. Gail's good cooking added to the festivities. Each summer, their father enjoyed leaving the heat of Maryland to spend a few weeks in the cool Alaskan climate.

One July, the father purchased a round trip ticket to Alaska. It cost several hundred dollars. Just before the departure date, the father had a heart attack and died. Gail called the airline to cancel the ticket. They refunded the money in a check made out to her father. She deposited the check to the joint account, and then closed out the account.

Once the bank received a certified copy of the death certificate, they gave Gail half of the balance of the account and the other half to Ken. Ken noticed that there was no recent deposit to his Dad's savings account and he wondered what happened to the money from the airline tickets.

Gail explained "Dad paid for the tickets from the joint account, so I deposited the money back to that account. "

"Aren't you going to give me half?"

"Dad meant for me to have whatever was in that joint account. If he wanted you to have half of the money, he would have made you joint owner as well."

Ken didn't see it that way "That refund was part of Dad's Estate. It should have been deposited to his savings account to be divided equally between us. Are you going force me to argue this in court?"

Gail finally agreed to split the money with Ken, but the damage was done.

Gail complains that holidays are lonely since Dad died.

LOCATING FINANCIAL RECORDS

To locate the decedent's assets you need to find evidence of what he owned and where those assets are located. His financial records should lead you to the location of all of his assets so your first job is to locate those records. The best place to start the search is in the decedent's home. Many people keep their financial records in a single place but it is important to check the entire house to be sure you did not miss something.

CHECK THE COMPUTER

Don't overlook that computer sitting silently in the corner. It may hold the decedent's check register and all of the decedent's financial records. The computer may be programmed to protect information. If you cannot access the decedent's records, you may need to employ a computer technician or computer consultant who will be able to print out all of the information on the hard drive of the computer. You can find such a technician or consultant by looking in the telephone book under

COMPUTER SUPPORT SERVICES or
COMPUTER SYSTEM DESIGNS & CONSULTANTS.

LOCATE TITLE TO MOTOR VEHICLE

If you are unable to locate the original Certificate of Title to the decedent's car, you can get a duplicate from the Motor Vehicle Administration ("MVA"). A surviving spouse can get a copy of title held jointly by the couple by taking a copy of the death certificate to the nearest full service branch office. In all other cases, the Personal Representative must make the request. It is a good idea to call your local MVA to determine what information they require and the cost of obtaining a replacement Certificate of Title (currently $20). Their in-state toll-free number (800) 950-1682. For the hearing impaired call (800) 492-4574 TDD. Out of state call (301) 729-4550.

TITLE TO MOBILE HOMES

Mobile homes longer than 35 feet are not required to be titled or registered in the state of Maryland, however, some mobile owners choose to do so. If the decedent owned a mobile home, regardless of its size, you should try to locate a Certificate of Title. If you cannot find it, then you can contact the MVA to obtain a duplicate title in the same manner as with any motor vehicle.

TITLE TO BOATS

All motor boats used primarily in the state of Maryland must be titled and registered with the Maryland Department of Natural Resources, with the exception of vessels that are registered with the U.S. Coast Guard. If the decedent owned a boat that he used principally in the state of Maryland, then you should be able to locate the Maryland title and registration to the boat. If you cannot locate the title and registration, then you can call the Maryland Department of Natural Resources at (410) 260-8200 and apply for a duplicate title and registration.

When you apply for a duplicate title of a motor vehicle, ask them to let you know if there is a lien (i.e., monies owed) on the car. In the state of Maryland, if monies are owed on a motor vehicle (car or mobile home), the owner keeps possession of the original title, and a Notice of Security Interest is mailed to the Lender. When the loan is paid, the lender must mail the Security Interest document (the loan document) to the owner. Once a Notice of Security Interest is filed, the owner of the motor vehicle will not be able to sell or transfer the motor vehicle without the Certificate of Title and the Security Interest document. If you find that there was a loan on the motor vehicle, and you cannot locate the original Security Interest document, then you need to contact the lender to determine the loan balance.

Special Situation

THE LEASED CAR

You may find that the car is leased and not owned by the decedent. If so, contact the lessor and get a copy of the lease agreement. Once you have the lease, check to see whether the decedent had life insurance as part of the agreement. If he did, then the lease may now be paid in full. The Personal Representative (or next of kin, if no Probate is necessary) can send the death certificate to the leasing company with a copy of the contract and a letter requesting that the paid contract be transferred to the beneficiary who can use the car for the remainder of the leasing period, or take title to the car, whichever option is available under the lease agreement. If the lease is not paid in full upon the decedent's death, then arrangements need to be made to satisfy the terms of the agreement. See Chapter 6 for information about transferring a leased car.

LOCATE CONTRACTS

If the decedent belonged to a health club or gym, he may have prepaid for the year. Look for the club contract. It will give the terms of the agreement. If you cannot locate the contract then contact the company for a copy of the agreement. If the contract was prepaid, then determine whether the agreement provides for a refund for the unused portion.

SERVICE CONTRACT

Many people purchase appliance service contracts to have their appliances serviced in the event that an appliance should need repair. If the decedent had a security system then he may have had a service contract with a company to monitor the system and contact the police in the event of a break-in. If the decedent had a service contract, then you need to locate it and determine whether it can be assigned to the new owner of the property.

If the contract is assignable, the new owner can reimburse the decedent's estate for the unused portion. If the contract cannot be assigned, then once the property is transferred, try to obtain a refund for the unused portion of the contract.

Special Situation

DECEDENT'S RESIDENTIAL LEASE

If the decedent was renting his residence, then he may have a written lease agreement. It is important to locate the lease because the decedent's estate may be responsible for payments under the lease. If you cannot locate the lease, then ask the landlord for a copy. If the landlord reports that there was no written lease, then verify that the decedent was on a month to month basis and then work out a mutually agreeable time in which to vacate the premises.

If a written lease is in effect, then determine the end of the lease period, and whether there was a security deposit. Ask whether the landlord will agree to cancel the lease on the condition that the property is left in good condition. If the landlord says that the estate is responsible to pay the balance of the lease, then it is prudent to have an attorney review the lease to determine what rights and responsibilities remain now that the tenant is deceased.

☎ **LAWYER**

DECEDENT'S ONGOING BUSINESS

If the decedent was the sole owner of a business, or if he owned a partnership interest in a business, the Personal Representative needs to contact the company accountant to obtain the company's business records. If there is a company attorney, then the attorney may be able to assist in obtaining the records. If you are a beneficiary of the estate, consider consulting with your own attorney to determine what rights and responsibilities you may have in the business.

COLLECT DEEDS

Collect the deeds to all property owned by the decedent. Many people keep deeds in a safe deposit box. If you cannot find the deed in the decedent's home, then you need to determine whether he had a safe deposit box. If you know that the decedent owned real property (lot, residence, condominium, cooperative, time share, etc.) but you cannot locate the deed, then contact the Clerk of the Land Records section of the Circuit Court in the county where the property is located (Real Property 3-103). The Clerk can provide you with a certified copy of the last recorded deed.

You will need to identify the parcel of land by giving the Clerk the recording reference which consists of a Liber Number and Folio Number or its tax identification number. You can find this information on the last tax bill sent to the decedent. If you cannot find the last property tax bill, then call the local Department of Assessments and Taxation and they may be able to give you the information based on the property address. You can also obtain information about any Maryland property through the states Web site:

MARYLAND STATE DEPARTMENT OF
ASSESSMENTS AND TAXATION
http://www.dat.state.md.us/

You can use the same procedure if you cannot locate the deed to property owned by the decedent in another state, namely, check with the recording department in the county where the property is located. In some states the County Recorder or Registrar of Deeds is in charge of the recording department.

COLLECT TAX RECORDS

The decedent's final state and federal income tax returns need to be filed so you should locate all of his tax records for the past 3 years. If you cannot locate his prior tax records, check his personal telephone book and/or his personal bank register to see if he employed someone to prepare his taxes. If you can locate his tax preparer, then he/she should have a copy of those records.

If you are unable to locate the decedent's federal tax returns then they can be obtained from the IRS. The IRS will send copies of the decedent's tax filings to anyone who has a ***fiduciary relationship*** with the decedent. The IRS considers the following people to be a fiduciary:

- the person appointed as the Personal Representative of the decedent's estate
- the Successor Trustee of the decedent's trust
- if the person died intestate, (without a Will) then whoever is legally entitled to possession of the decedent's property (See Chapter 5 for an explanation of the Laws of Intestate Succession).

The fiduciary can receive copies of the decedent's tax filings by notifying IRS that he/she is acting in a fiduciary capacity, and then requesting the copies.

To notify the IRS of the fiduciary capacity file Form 56:
NOTICE CONCERNING FIDUCIARY RELATIONSHIP

To request the copies, file IRS Form 4506:
REQUEST FOR COPY OR TRANSCRIPT OF TAX FORM
Your accountant can file these forms for you or you can obtain the forms from the IRS by calling (800) 829-3676 or you can download them from the Internet:

IRS FORMS WEB SITE
http://www.irs.gov/forms_pubs/forms.html

LOCATE STATE INCOME TAX RETURN

If you cannot locate the decedent's state income tax return you can get a copy from the Comptroller of Maryland. If a Probate procedure is necessary, then the Personal Representative can get the copy. If no Probate is necessary, and you are next of kin, then you can request a copy by faxing a request to (410) 974-2967 or you can write to: COMPTROLLER OF MARYLAND
Central Files Division
Annapolis, MD 21411

You may be able to save time by first calling the Personal Income Tax Office to determine what information they may require. In state call (800) 638-2927. Out of state call (410) 260-7980.

LOCATE OUT OF STATE ACCOUNTS

If the decedent had out of state bank or brokerage accounts, then you might be able to locate them if they mail out monthly or quarterly statements. Not all financial institutions do so, but all institutions are required to send out an IRS tax form 1099 each year giving the amount of interest earned on that account. Once the forms come in, you will learn the location of all of the decedent's active accounts.

If the decedent was forgetful, he may have money in a lost bank account or abandoned safe deposit box. Property that is unclaimed is turned over to the Maryland State Comptroller. The time period for turning abandoned bank accounts, unclaimed wages, utility deposits, insurance proceeds and most other items is 5 years but it could vary depending on the item. For example, a travelers check is not considered abandoned until 15 years from the date of issue have passed.

Before turning the property over to the state, the holder of the unclaimed property must make a good faith effort to contact the owner and return the property to the owner. Once the property is turned over to the state, the Comptroller will publish a notice entitled "Notice of Names Of Persons Appearing To Be Owners Of Abandoned Property" in a newspaper of general circulation in the area of the last known address of the owner of the property.

If a tangible item (such as jewelry) remains unclaimed, the Comptroller will convert it to cash by holding a public auction. Up to $50,000 of the proceeds of the sale are placed in the Maryland Legal Services Corporation to provide for legal services for the poor. The remaining funds go to the General Fund of the state.

There is no time limit on claiming funds. If the item is later claimed, the Comptroller will give the proceeds of the sale to the owner (or his heir), plus interest, up to 5 years, for the period the Administrator held the property (Commercial Law 17-101, 17-301, 17-302, 17-303, 17-308, 17-311, 17-314, 17-316, 17-317).

You can determine whether there is a record identifying the decedent as the owner of abandoned property in Maryland by calling the Comptroller of Maryland at (800) 782-7383, or by visiting their Web site at:

COMPTROLLER OF MARYLAND
http://www.comp.state.md.us/

CLAIMS IN OTHER STATES

Each state has an agency or department that is responsible for handling lost, abandoned or unclaimed property located within that state. If the decedent had residences in other states, then call the UNCLAIMED or ABANDONED PROPERTY department of the state Comptroller or Treasurer to see if the decedent has unclaimed property in that state. EAGLE PUBLISHING COMPANY OF BOCA lists telephone numbers for the unclaimed property division for each state at their Web site:

EAGLE PUBLISHING COMPANY OF BOCA
http://www.eaglepublishing.com

CLAIMS FOR DECEDENT VICTIMS OF HOLOCAUST

The New York State Banking Department has a special Claims Processing Office for Holocaust survivors or their heirs. The office processes claims for Swiss bank accounts that were dormant since the end of World War II. If the decedent was a victim of the Holocaust, you can get information about money that may be due to the decedent's estate by calling (800) 695-3318.

CLAIMS FOR IRS TAX REFUNDS

The IRS reports that some 90,000 tax refund checks representing 67.4 million dollars were returned to them as being not deliverable. They keep the information on file and will forward the full amount once they locate the taxpayer. You can determine whether they are holding a check for the decedent by calling the IRS at (800) 829-1040.

FILING THE WILL

Anyone who has possession of the decedent's original Will is required to deposit it with the Register of Wills in the county of the decedent's residence. If the decedent owned property in Maryland, but did not live here, then the Will needs to be deposited with the Register in the county where most of the decedent's property is located (Est. & Trusts 5-101, 5-103). Anyone who has the Will and who willfully fails or refuses to deposit the Will with the Register after being notified of the death, can be sued for any loss suffered because of that failure or refusal (Est. & Trusts 4-202).

The Register of Wills will accept an original Will only and not a copy, so it is important to hand carry the original document to the Register. If you are the Personal Representative of the Will, you can give it to your attorney to file with the court as part of the Probate procedure. Make a copy of the Will for your own records before delivering it to the Register or to your attorney.

Special Situation

WILL DRAFTED IN ANOTHER STATE OR COUNTRY

A Will that was drafted in another state or country can be accepted into Probate in Maryland, provided:

☑ the Will is in writing, and it was

☑ signed by the decedent according to the laws of the state where it was drafted - or - to the laws of Maryland - or - to the laws of the state where the decedent had his residence (Est. & Trusts 4-104).

In Maryland, a Will is considered to be properly signed if the decedent signed the Will in the presence of two creditable witnesses (Est. & Trust 4-102).

☎ LAWYER

OUT OF STATE PROPERTY OR RESIDENCE

If the decedent had his residence in Maryland and owned property in another state, then you may need to have an initial Probate procedure in Maryland and an ***ancillary*** (secondary) Probate procedure in the other state. If the decedent had his residence in another state and owned property in Maryland, then it may need to be done the other way around; namely, you may need to conduct the initial Probate in the other state. Maryland law does not require that Letters be issued in this state. Letters issued in the other state are sufficient to conduct Probate business here in Maryland, however the Personal Representative needs to follow Maryland law as it relates to the transfer of property within the state (Est. & Trusts 5-501, 5-502).

If you are going to be Personal Representative, and the decedent owned property in another state or was a resident of another state, then before depositing the Will with the Court you should consult with an experienced Probate attorney in each state to determine where the initial Probate should be conducted. Convenience is an important consideration, but you also need to consider that each state has its own tax structure and Probate statutes. Ask each attorney whether the location of the initial Probate procedure will have any effect on the total cost of the Probate procedure, who is to inherit the property or how much the estate will be taxed.

THE MISSING WILL

People tend to put off making a Will until they think they need to. For many, that need arises when they are elderly and/or seriously ill and have assets that they want to leave to someone. Young people with few assets usually do not have a Will. People who are aged and with significant assets usually have a Will or Trust. A survey conducted for the American Association of Retired Persons ("AARP") found that the probability of having a Will increases with age. Forty-four percent of those surveyed who were between the ages of 50 to 54 had a Will. This increased to 85% for those who were 80 and older. You can find more details of the survey at their Web site:

AARP WEB SITE
http://research.aarp.org

Those who make a Will, usually tell the person that they appoint as Executor, of the existence of the Will. Chances are, that someone in the decedent's circle of family and friends, knows whether there is a Will. If you believe that the decedent had a Will, but you cannot find it, then there are at least three places to check out:

⇨ THE DECEDENT'S ATTORNEY

Look at the decedent's checkbook for the past few years and see whether he paid any attorney fees. If you are able to locate the decedent's attorney, then call and inquire whether the attorney ever drafted a Will for the decedent, and if so, whether the attorney has the original Will in his possession. If he has the Will, then ask him to forward it to the Register of Wills in the county of the decedent's residence. Asking the attorney to forward the Will to the court does not obligate you to employ the attorney should you later find that you need the assistance of an attorney for the Probate administration.

➪ THE REGISTER OF WILLS

Maryland law gives residents the right to deposit their Will with the Register of Wills in the county of their residence. Check with the Register of Wills in the Probate Court in any county where the decedent lived. If the decedent lived in Baltimore, then check with the Baltimore Orphan's Court. If the Will is on file, the Register will keep the Will until it is offered for Probate. The Register will notify the Personal Representative, and anyone else that the Register thinks appropriate to notify, that the Will is on deposit (Est. & Trusts 4-201).

➪ THE SAFE DEPOSIT BOX

Most people keep their original Will in a safe deposit box. If you believe that the decedent had a Will but you cannot find it, then check to see if the decedent had a safe deposit box. If he did, you will need to gain entry to that box to see whether the Will is in the box. See the next page for an explanation of how to gain entry to the safe deposit box.

☎ LAWYER A COPY BUT NO ORIGINAL

A person can revoke his Will simply by destroying it (Est. & Trusts 4-105). If you have a copy of the Will and cannot find the original, the Registrar will presume that the decedent revoked that Will. If you believe the original was lost and not revoked, you can ask the Probate Court to admit the copy to Probate. You will need to prove that the copy is a true copy of the original and that the decedent had no intention of revoking that Will. These are not easy things to prove. You will need to employ an attorney experienced in Probate matters to present your case to the Court.

ACCESSING THE SAFE DEPOSIT BOX

If the decedent rented a safe deposit box with another person, each with free access to the box, then the surviving joint renter of the box can go to the box and remove the contents of the box. If the decedent had a safe deposit in his name alone and you think his Will may be in the safe deposit box, you can ask the Lessor of the box (usually a bank) to let you inspect the box to see whether the Will is there. Under Maryland law, the Lessor may allow you to see the contents of the box under the supervision of an officer or employee of the company (Finan. Inst. 12-603).

If the Will is there, the Lessor can arrange to have it delivered to the Register of Wills. You may save yourself time and hassle, if you first call the financial institution and make an appointment to meet with an officer. Ask what identification they will require of you. Most will want to see the death certificate.

Other than the Will, nothing else can be removed from the safe deposit box until a Personal Representative is appointed. Whether or not the Will is in the box, it is a good idea to take an inventory of the items contained within the box. If there needs to be a Probate procedure, then the Personal Representative can gain access to the safe deposit box as soon as he obtains his Letters.

Once you have located all of the decedent's property you may think the next step is to determine who gets to inherit that property. But some of that property may be needed to pay monies owed by the decedent; so the next step is to determine what, if any, bills need to be paid. And that is the topic of the next chapter.

What Bills Need To Be Paid? 4

The Personal Representative has the duty to be sure that all valid ***claims against the estate*** (demand for payment) are paid. If the decedent had debts, but no money or property, then of course, there is no way to pay the claim. The only remaining question is whether anyone else is responsible to pay the decedent's debts. If the decedent was married, then the first person the creditor will look to, is the decedent's spouse. To understand the basis of this expectation, you need to know a bit of the history of our legal system.

Our laws are derived from English Common Law. Under early English Common Law, a single woman had the right to own property in her own name and also the right to contract to buy or sell property; but when she married, her legal identity merged with her spouse. She could not hold property free from her husband's claim or control. She could no longer enter into a contract without her husband's permission.

Once married, a woman became financially dependent on her husband. He, in turn, became legally responsible to provide his wife with basic necessities — food, clothing, shelter and medical services. If anyone provided basic necessities to his wife, then, regardless of whether the husband agreed to be responsible for the debt, he became obliged to pay for them. This law was called the DOCTRINE OF NECESSARIES.

States in America departed from English Common Law by enacting a series of Married Women's Rights Acts giving a married woman the right to own property and to contract in her own name.

In the United States, a series of Married Women's Rights Acts were passed giving a married woman the right to own property. After these laws were passed, cases followed that tested whether the Doctrine of Necessaries still applied. Judges had to decide:

> *If a wife can own property and contract to pay for her own necessaries, should her husband be responsible for her debts, in the event that she does not have enough money to pay for them?*

For those states deciding to continue to hold the husband liable, a second question to be decided was:

> *If the husband is responsible for his wife's necessaries, should she be responsible for his?*

In some states, notably Florida, courts decided that neither partner was responsible to pay the other's necessities, unless they contracted or agreed to do so. In Maryland, the Court of Appeals refused to rule on the issue saying that it was something the legislature needed to decide (*Condor v. Prince George's County, Maryland*, 289 Md. 516 (1981), 425 A.2d 1011).

The Maryland legislature responded to the invitation and in 1989 repealed Family Law 4-302 which was the Maryland Doctrine of Necessaries. Under current Maryland law neither partner is responsible to pay for the necessaries of the other. If the spouse who made the contract or purchase, does not have sufficient funds to pay, then his/her spouse is not responsible for the debt unless the spouse agrees to do so (Family Law 4-301). An exception to this law is the case of a married person who receives Public Assistance for his health care needs. Under Maryland law, the spouse is responsible to reimburse the state for monies spent to the extent that the spouse is able to pay (Health-Gen 15-122).

JOINT DEBTS

A ***joint debt*** is a debt that two or more people are responsible to pay. Usually the contract or promissory note reads that both parties agree to ***joint and several*** liability, meaning they both agree to pay the debt and each of them, individually, agree to be pay the debt. A joint debt can also be in the form of monies owed by one person with payment guaranteed by another person. If the person who owes the money does not pay, then the ***guarantor*** (the person who guaranteed payment) is responsible to make payment. Hospital bills, nursing home bills, funeral expenses, legal fees incurred because of the decedent's death are all debts of the decedent's estate. They are not joint debts unless someone guaranteed payment for monies owed.

PAYING FOR THE JOINT DEBT

If another person is jointly responsible for monies owed by the decedent, then that bill should be paid from any joint account held with the decedent. If the joint debtor did not have a joint account with the decedent, then the joint debtor must pay the bill from his/her own funds.

SPOUSE

JOINT SPOUSAL DEBTS

Loans signed by the decedent and his spouse are joint debts, as are charges on credit cards that both were authorized to use. Property taxes are a joint debt if the decedent and the spouse both owned the property. Also, if the decedent was receiving Public Assistance for his health care needs, then the spouse remains liable to reimburse the state for monies spent.

JOINT PROPERTY BUT NO JOINT DEBT

Suppose all of the decedent's funds are held jointly with a family member and the joint owner of the bank account did not agree to pay those debts? Can the creditor require that half of the joint funds be set aside to pay the debt?

The answer depends on how the account was set up. When a bank account is established the owners of the account sign an agreement with the bank stating who is to receive the funds should one of the joint owners die. Unless the agreement says differently, if one of the owners of a joint account dies, then those remaining own the account (Finan. Instit. 1-204). Unless the surviving owner(s) agreed to pay for the decedent's debt, the creditor cannot require that any of the joint funds be used to pay the debt.

NO EXEMPTION FOR TAXES

The beneficiary of the decedent's joint account has no obligation to use the joint account funds to pay the decedent's creditors; however, the decedent's share of the joint account is included as part of the decedent's **Taxable** Estate. If federal or state taxes are due, whoever takes the decedent's share of the joint account may be required to pay whatever taxes are due on the decedent's share of the account. But if the decedent gave instructions in his Will that all his taxes are to be paid from monies set aside for that purpose, the Personal Representative will follow those directions and pay the taxes (Tax-Gen. 7-308).

NO MONEY — NO PROPERTY

If the decedent owed money then the debt needs to be paid from assets owned by the decedent — which leads to the next question "Did the decedent have any money in his own name when he died?"

If the decedent died without any money or property in his name, then there is no money to pay any creditor. The only question that remains is whether anyone else is liable to pay those bills. The issue of payment most often arises in relation to services provided by nursing homes. When a person enters a nursing home, he is usually too ill to speak for himself or even sign his name. In such cases, the nursing home administrator will ask the spouse or a family member to sign a battery of papers on behalf of the patient before allowing the patient to enter the facility. Buried in that battery of papers may be a statement that the family member agrees to be responsible for payment to the nursing home. If the family member refuses to guarantee payment and the patient's finances are limited, then the facility may refuse to admit the patient.

If a nursing home accepts Medicare or Medicaid payments, then, under the Federal Nursing Home Reform Law, the nursing home is prohibited from requiring a family member to guarantee payment as a condition of allowing the patient to enter that facility (USC Title 42 §1395I-3(c)(5)(A)(ii)). Maryland law has similar prohibitions (Health-Gen. 19-344). Nonetheless, it is common practice for a nursing home, in effect, to say "Either someone agrees to pay for the patient's bill or you need to find a different facility."

Their position is understandable, in light of the fact that even if the patient is married, the nursing home cannot require payment from the spouse unless the spouse agrees to be responsible for monies owed. Most nursing homes are business establishments and not charitable organizations. The nursing home must be paid for the services they provide or they soon will be out of business. For an insolvent patient, the solution to the problem is to have the patient admitted to a facility as a Medicaid patient.

But suppose the decedent had some money when he entered the nursing home and you agreed to guarantee payment to the nursing home?

What if you feel that you were coerced into signing as a guarantor?

Are you now liable to pay the decedent's final nursing home bill if your family member died without funds?

An experienced Elder Law attorney will be able to answer these questions after examining the documents that you signed and the conditions under which the patient entered the nursing home.

PAYING THE DECEDENT'S BILLS

If the decedent was married and no Probate procedure is necessary, then the surviving spouse needs to make provision for paying bills they were both responsible to pay. If the decedent was not married and he owned property belonging to him alone, such as a bank account, securities or real property, then paying monies owed by the decedent falls to the Personal Representative.

Just as soon as he is appointed, the Personal Representative is required to make a diligent effort to locate all of the decedent's creditors and notify them that they have two months to file a claim against the decedent's estate. Any creditor who is not given notice has 6 months from the date of death to come forward and present his claim (Est. & Trusts 7-103.1).

The Personal Representative needs to look over each claim and decide whether that claim is valid. The problem with making that decision is that the decedent is not here to say whether he actually received the goods and services that are now being billed to his estate.

That is especially the case for medical or nursing care bills. An example of improper billing brought to the attention of this author was that of a bill submitted for a physical examination of the decedent. The bill listed the date of the examination as July 10th, but the decedent died on July 9th. Other incorrect billings may not be as obvious, so each invoice needs to be carefully examined.

If the Personal Representative decides to challenge a bill, and is unable to settle the matter with the creditor, then the Probate court will decide whether the debt is valid and should be paid.

MEDICAL BILLS COVERED BY INSURANCE

If the decedent had health insurance you may receive an invoice stamped "THIS IS NOT A BILL." This means the health care provider has submitted the bill to the decedent's health insurance company and expects to be paid by them. Even though payment is not requested, it is important to verify that the bill is valid for two reasons:

➢ LATER LIABILITY

If the insurer refuses to pay the claim, the facility will seek payment from whoever is in possession of the decedent's property, and that may reduce the amount inherited by the beneficiaries.

➢ INCREASED HEALTH CARE COSTS

Regardless of whether the decedent was covered by a private health care insurer or Medicare, improper billing increases the cost of health insurance to all of us. Consumers pay high premiums for health coverage. We, as taxpayers, all share the cost of Medicare. If unnecessary or fraudulent billing is not checked, then ultimately, we all pay.

Special Situation MEDICARE FRAUD

If you believe that you have come across a case of Medicare fraud, you can call the ANTI-FRAUD HOTLINE (800)447-8477 and report the incident to the Office of the Inspector General of the United States Department of Health and Human Services.

HOW TO CHECK MEDICARE BILLING

If the decedent was covered by Medicare, then an important billing question is whether the health care provider agreed to accept Medicare ***assignment of benefits***, meaning that they agreed to accept payment directly from Medicare. If so, the maximum liability for the patient is **20%** of the amount determined as reasonable by Medicare. For example, suppose a doctor bills Medicare $1,000 for medical treatment of the decedent. If Medicare determines that a reasonable fee is $800, then the patient is liable for 20% of the $800 ($160).

Health care providers who do not accept Medicare assignment bill the patient directly. They can charge up to 15% more than the amount allowed by Medicare. If the decedent knew and agreed to be liable for the payment, then his estate may be liable for whatever Medicare doesn't pay. For example, if a doctor's bill is $1,000 and Medicare allows $800, then Medicare will reimburse the decedent's estate 80% of $800 ($640). The doctor may charge the estate 15% more than the $800 ($920) and the estate may be liable for the difference: $920 - $640 or $280.

To summarize:
For health care providers accepting Medicare assignment, the most they can bill the decedent's estate is 20% of what Medicare allows (not 20% of what they bill.)

Those who do not accept Medicare assignment, can bill 15% more than the amount allowed by Medicare. The decedent's estate may be liable for the difference between the amount billed and the amount paid by Medicare.

In either case, if the decedent had secondary health care insurance, then the secondary insurer may be responsible to pay for the difference.

Special Situation

DENIAL OF MEDICARE COVERAGE

If the health care provider reports to you that a service provided to the decedent is not covered by Medicare, or if the facility submits the bill to Medicare and Medicare refuses to pay, then check to see if you agree with that ruling by determining what services are covered under Medicare. See page 45 of this book for information about how to obtain a pamphlet that explains what medical treatments are covered under Medicare. If you have specific billing questions about Part A, you can call Blue Cross Blue Shield of Maryland at (800) 655-1636. For Part B questions call Trailblazer Health Enterprises (800) 444-4606. For the hearing impaired call TTY/ TDD (877) 486-2048.

APPEALING THE DECISION

If you believe that the decedent was wrongly denied coverage, then you can appeal that decision. The State Health Insurance Program ("SHIP") can explain how to go about filing a Medicare appeal. You can call the Maryland Department of Aging at (800) 243-3425 for a referral to the SHIP office nearest you.

If you want an attorney to assist with your appeal, call the Maryland Bar at (800) 492-1964 for a referral to an attorney experienced in Medicare appeals. Some attorneys work ***pro bono*** (literally for the public good; i.e. without charge) but most charge to assist in an appeal. Federal statute 42 U.S.C. §406(a)(2)(A) limits the amount an attorney may charge for a successful Medicare appeal to 25% of the amount recovered or $4,000, whichever is the smaller amount.

Special Situation

DECEDENT ON MEDICAID

Medicaid is a program that provides medical and long term nursing care for people with low income and limited resources. The program is funded jointly by the federal and state government. Federal law requires the state to recover monies spent from the estate of a Medicaid recipient who was 55 or older when the decedent received Medicaid assistance. The state will seek reimbursement for the cost of nursing home care or for home based care or for other community based services. Federal law prohibits any recovery of monies spent, until the surviving spouse, and/or disabled child of the decedent are deceased (42 U.S.C. 1396(p), Health-Gen 15-121).

Even if the Medicaid recipient is single, there usually is no money to recover because to qualify for a Public Assistance Program in Maryland, a person must have limited income and assets. The amount varies with the size of the family and type of program. To participate in a medical assistance program, at this time, a single person may not have assets that exceed $2,500.

Sometimes it happens that a person on Medicaid or other Public Assistance Program dies and his estate later receives money perhaps as part of a settlement of a lawsuit. In such case, a Probate procedure will be necessary and the state will file a claim for reimbursement of monies spent by the state on behalf of the decedent (MC 88A-77). If you have a question about the claim you can call the Division of Medical Assistance Recoveries at (410) 767-1787.

SOME THINGS ARE CREDITOR PROOF

Sometimes it happens that the decedent had money or property titled in his name only, but he also had a significant amount of debt. In such cases the beneficiaries may wonder whether they should go through a Probate procedure if there will be little, if anything, left after the creditors are paid. Before making the decision consider that some assets are protected under Maryland law:

✧ LIFE INSURANCE PROCEEDS ✧

The spouse, child or dependent relative of the decedent can receive the proceeds of a life insurance policy or annuity contract free from the claims of the decedent's creditors. There is no creditor protection if the proceeds are paid to any other beneficiary or to the decedent's estate (Est. & Trusts 8-115, Insur. 16-111).

✧ BENEFITS FROM A FRATERNAL BENEFIT SOCIETY ✧

Any benefit that is payable by a fraternal benefit society (e.g., AARP, American Legion, Kiwanis, Lighthouse for the Blind, Rotary Club, etc.) is free of the monies owed by the decedent. In fact, benefits paid by a fraternal benefit society are free from the claims of the creditors of the member of the society AND from the creditors of the beneficiary (Est. & Trusts 8-115, Insur. 8-431).

✧ ILLNESS OR INJURY PROCEEDS ✧

Any money paid as a result of the decedent's illness, injury, accident, or death is exempt from the claims of the decedent's creditors. This includes money payable as a result of an arbitration, judgment, insurance or other compensation (Courts & Jud. Proc. 11-504).

✧ PENSION PLANS ✧

Annuities, pensions, profit sharing or other retirement plans regulated by the federal Employee Retirement Income Security Act of 1974 ("ERISA"), including IRA accounts and plans identified by the Internal Revenue Code as 401(a) and 403(a & b), 408, 408A, 414(d & e) and 409 as in effect prior to January, 1984, are creditor proof. Monies received by a beneficiary of such plans are protected from the decedent's creditors with some qualifications:

NO EXEMPTION FOR TAXES

In general, income taxes are not paid when money is placed in a retirement plan. Taxes are paid when the monies are withdrawn from the account regardless of whether the monies are withdrawn by the retiree or the person he named as beneficiary of the retirement plan. If you are inheriting money from the decedent's pension, retirement allowance, or annuity, then you may need to pay taxes on those monies. You should consult with an accountant or an attorney to determine how much money needs to be set aside to pay for federal and state income taxes.

NO EXEMPTION FOR PUBLIC ASSISTANCE CLAIMS

If the decedent was receiving assistance under a Maryland Public Assistance Program, the Maryland Department of Health and Mental Hygiene has the right to file a claim against the decedent's estate for monies spent on his behalf. If no Probate procedure is necessary, the state has the right to require payment from the decedent's pension plan (Courts & Jud. Proc. 11-504).

✧ THERE IS A PRIORITY OF PAYMENT ✧

Next, consider that not all Probate debts are equal. If there are insufficient funds in the Probate Estate to pay for all claims against the decedent's estate, then Maryland Statute (Est. & Trusts 8-105) establishes an order of priority for payment:

CLASS 1: FEES TO REGISTER

Top priority goes to any fees charged by the Register of Wills for their work in administering the Probate Estate. The current fee for estates between $100,000 and $250,000 is $400. But fees range from $50 for estates that are less than $10,000 going up to $2,500 + .02% of amounts in excess of 5 million dollars (Est. & Trusts 2-206).

CLASS 2: COST OF ADMINISTRATION

Second in priority is any cost or expense associated with the administration of the estate. This includes accounting and appraisal fees, but not Personal Representative or attorney fees, which are a Class 4 expense.

CLASS 3: FUNERAL EXPENSES

Anyone who paid for the decedent's funeral is entitled to be reimbursed. Up to $5,000 of that expense is a Class 3 debt. Anything over that value becomes a Class 8 claim, unless the Court rules otherwise (Est. & Trusts 8-106).

CLASS 4: PERSONAL REPRESENTATIVE FEES

Fourth in line for payment are the Personal Representative fees, attorney fees, and commissions due to a licensed real estate broker for the sale of the decedent's real property. The Personal Representative's fees are regulated by Maryland statute (see Page 144 for an explanation of the law).

CLASS 5: FAMILY ALLOWANCE

If the decedent was survived by a spouse and/or minor child, then they are entitled to a Family Allowance for their maintenance during the Probate procedure. The spouse is entitled to an allowance of $5,000. Each unmarried child under the age of 18 is entitled to receive $2,500 (Est. & Trusts 3-201).

CLASS 6: TAXES

Taxes owed by the decedent (or his estate) are a class 6 debt.

CLASS 7: MEDICAL, HOSPITAL and NURSING EXPENSES

Seventh in line for payment are the reasonable expenses of the decedent's last illness. This includes medical, hospital and nursing home expenses.

CLASS 8: RENT

Up to three months of back rent owed by the decedent is a Class 8 debt.

CLASS 9: WAGES

Monies owed by the decedent as payment for wages, salaries, or commissions for work done for the decedent up to 3 months prior to his death are a class 9 debt.

CLASS 10: PUBLIC ASSISTANCE CLAIMS

Monies spent by the state of Maryland on the decedent as a recipient of a State Public Assistance program such as Medicaid, is a Class 10 claim (MC 88A-77).

CLASS 11: ALL OTHER CLAIMS

There is no preference of payment within a given class. If there is not sufficient money to pay everyone in a given class, then whatever money is available is prorated among them.

✧ THERE IS A STATUTE OF LIMITATIONS ✧

There are federal and state laws that set time periods for pursuing a claim. Anyone who wishes to take court action must do so within the time set by the given Statute of Limitation. For example, in Maryland, the Statute of Limitation for bringing suit against a doctor for malpractice is 5 years from the date of injury, or 3 years from the date of discovery of the injury, whichever is the shorter period (Courts & Jud. Proc. 5-109). Civil actions involving the sale of securities must be brought within 1 year of the violation or the discovery of the violation, but not later than 3 years from the date of sale (Corps. & Ass'ns 11-703). Time periods can be extended under certain circumstances, but in general, if the person does not sue within the period set by the Statute of Limitations, they lose the right to pursue the claim.

Once a person dies, any suit for slander against the decedent's estate cannot be pursued, even if the suit was filed against the decedent before his death. Any other claim against the decedent's estate must be filed within 6 months from the date of death. If the Personal Representative sends the creditor notice of the death in the form required by Maryland statute (Est. & Trusts 7-103), then that period is shortened to 2 months from date of delivery of the notice. If someone files a claim against the estate and the Statute of Limitation for that claim has passed, then the Personal Representative is under no duty to pay that claim.

As explained on Page 87, it may happen that monies come into the decedent's estate long after his death. In such case the state of Maryland has 6 months from the date that a Personal Representative is appointed, or 2 months after receiving notice, to file a claim to recover monies spent on behalf of the decedent as a recipient of the Maryland Medical Assistance Program (Est. & Trusts 8-103).

☎ LAWYER

DECEDENT LEAVING CONSIDERABLE DEBT

If the decedent died leaving much debt and no property, then the solution is simple. No Probate, no one gets paid. But if the decedent had property and died owing more money than the property was worth, his heirs may decide that going through a Probate procedure is just not worth the effort, or they may decide to simply wait out the 6 month Statute of Limitation period and begin Probate at that time.

This may not be the best decision. Some creditors are tenacious and will use whatever legal strategy is available in order to be paid, including initiating the Probate procedure themselves. If no one starts a Probate procedure, then a creditor can petition the court to be appointed as Personal Representative of the estate (Est. & Trusts 5-104).

Family members may object to having a creditor as a Personal Representative, so there could be a court battle over who has priority to be appointed as Personal Representative. Court battles are expensive, emotionally as well as financially. Before you decide to distance yourself from the Probate procedure, consult with an attorney experienced in Probate matters for an opinion about the best way to administer the estate.

MONIES OWED TO THE DECEDENT

Suppose you owed money to the decedent. Do you need to pay that debt now that he is dead? That depends on whether there is some written document that says the debt is forgiven once the decedent dies. For example, suppose the decedent lent you money to buy your home. If he left a Will saying that once he dies, your debt is forgiven, then you do not need to make any more payments. If you signed a promissory note and mortgage at the time you borrowed the money from the decedent, then the Persona Representative should sign the original promissory note "PAID IN FULL" and return the note to you. If the mortgage was recorded, then the Personal Representative should sign and record a satisfaction of mortgage in the land records of the Circuit Court.

If you owed the decedent money and there is no Will, or if there is a Will, no mention of forgiving the debt, then you still owe the money. Monies borrowed from the decedent and his spouse need to be repaid to the spouse. Monies borrowed from the decedent only, become an asset to the estate of the decedent, meaning that you owe the money to the decedent's estate. If you are one of the beneficiaries of the estate, you can deduct the money from your inheritance.

For example, suppose your father left $70,000 in a bank account to be divided equally between you and your two brothers. If you owed your father $20,000, then your father's estate is really worth $90,000. Instead of paying the $20,000, you can agree to receive $10,000 and have the $20,000 debt forgiven. Each of your brothers will then receive $30,000 in cash.

Who Are The Beneficiaries? 5

A question that comes up early on is who is entitled to the property of the decedent. To answer the question you first need to know how the property was titled (owned) as of the date of death.

There are three ways to own property. The decedent could have owned property jointly with another person; or in trust for another person; or the decedent could have owned property that was titled in his name only.

In general, upon the decedent's death:

> Property held as **Joint Tenants** belongs to the surviving joint owner(s).
>
> **Trust Property** belongs to the beneficiary of the Trust.
>
> Property owned by the **decedent only** is inherited by the beneficiaries named in the Will. If there is no Will, then the property goes to his heirs according to Maryland's Laws of Intestate Succession
>
> NOTE ➪ If the decedent was married, then his spouse may have rights in his property.

This chapter explains each of these types of ownership in detail.

PROPERTY HELD JOINTLY

Bank accounts, securities, motor vehicles, real property can all be owned jointly by two or more people. If one of the joint owners dies, then the survivor(s) own the property.

THE JOINT BANK ACCOUNT

When a person opens a bank or credit union account in Maryland, he signs an ***Account Agreement*** with the bank stating who has access to the account, and how the funds in the account should be distributed in the event that the owner of the account dies (Finan. Instit. 1-204). If two people set up a ***joint account,*** then should one of the owners of the account die, the account belongs to the remaining owner.

If a joint account is held in three names and one owner dies, then either surviving owner can go to the bank and withdraw all of the funds in the account. With such an arrangement, the surviving owners need to cooperate with each other to divide the funds in the account equitably. The surviving owner(s) need to keep in mind that the decedent's share of the account must be used to pay the prorata share of the decedent's estate taxes (see page 80).

If the last surviving owner of a joint account dies, then unless the Account Agreement states otherwise, the money in the account becomes part of the decedent's Probate estate and will go to whomever he named in his Will as the beneficiary of the property. If there is no Will, then the decedent's share goes to his next of kin as defined in Maryland Laws of Intestate Succession (see page 109).

THE CONVENIENCE ACCOUNT

The decedent may have set up a Convenience Account and given someone (his ***Agent*** or ***Convenience Person***) authority to make bank transactions on his behalf. The Agent or Convenience Person does not own any of the monies in the account, and should not add to or withdraw from the account once the owner of the account dies. The bank will transfer the funds according to the terms of Account Agreement signed by the decedent (Finan. Instit. 1-204).

A bank statement or a pass book may not give all of the details of the terms of the bank account, so it is important to actually read the Account Agreement to determine how the account funds should be distributed now that the owner of the account is deceased.

JOINTLY HELD SECURITIES

You can usually determine whether the decedent owns a security alone or jointly with another by examining the face of the stock or bond certificate. If two names are printed on the certificate as Joint Tenants, then the surviving joint owner now owns the security. Each state has its own securities regulations. If the security was registered or purchased in another state you might see two names on the certificate followed by "JTWRS." The initials stand for "Joint Tenants With Rights of Survivorship." This is the same as a Maryland Joint Tenancy. The surviving owner can either cash in the security or ask the company to issue a new certificate in the name of the surviving owner, again understanding that the surviving owner(s) may need to contribute their prorata share of the decedent's estate taxes.

If the security is in two names with no indication of whether it is a Joint Tenancy, then you will need to contact the company to determine how the account was set up.

If the decedent held a motor vehicle jointly with his spouse, then the surviving spouse now owns the motor vehicle. The surviving spouse can have title to the property changed to his/her name only, by taking the original certificate of title and a certified copy of the death certificate to the nearest full service branch office of the Motor Vehicle Administration ("MVA"). If monies are owed on the car, the surviving spouse will need to get a release from the lender before the MVA will allow the transfer; i.e., the surviving spouse will need the original Security Interest document in order to make the transfer.

Other than a married couple, in Maryland, joint ownership of a motor vehicle is a ***Tenancy-In-Common*** meaning that there is no right of survivorship. If one joint owner dies his "half" goes to whoever he named in his Will. If he died without a Will, then his share goes to whoever inherits his property under Maryland's Laws of Intestate Succession.

MOTOR VEHICLE IN DECEDENT'S NAME ONLY

The same applies if the decedent's car was in his name only. In such case, the car goes to the beneficiaries named in the Will. If the decedent died without a Will then the car goes to the next of kin defined in the Maryland Laws of Intestate Succession. See page 109 for an explanation of the law.

See Chapter 6 for an explanation of how to transfer title of the motor vehicle to the proper beneficiary.

MARYLAND REAL PROPERTY HELD JOINTLY

The name of the owner of real property is printed on the face of the deed. To determine whether the decedent owned the property jointly with another person, you need to look at the last recorded deed. See page 67 if you cannot locate the deed. The first paragraph of the deed should identify the present owner of the property. For example:

> This Deed made the 14th day of August, 2000
> by ROBERT TRAYNOR, a single man
> party of the first part, and
> SUSAN CODY, a married woman
> and HENRY TRAYNOR, a single man,
> party of the second part, **in joint tenancy**
> Witnesseth, that in consideration for $95,000
> the said party of the first part conveys
> to the parties of the second part,
> their heirs and assigns, in fee simple . . .
> the following described real property . . .

Robert Traynor (the party of the first part) is the ***Grantor*** of the deed. He transferred the property to Susan Cody and Henry Traynor (parties of the second part) who are the ***Grantees*** and the present owners of the property. Robert transferred the property to Susan and Henry in ***joint tenancy*** meaning that should one of them die, the other owns the property 100%. Nothing need be done to establish the ownership, but both names remain on the deed. The surviving owner needs to keep a certified copy of the death certificate to present at closing when the property is transferred to show that there just one owner.

DEED WITH A LIFE ESTATE

A ***life estate*** interest in real property means that the person who owns the life estate has the right to live in that property until he/she dies. You can identify a life estate interest by examining the face of the deed. If somewhere on the face of the deed you see the phrase WITH A LIFE ESTATE TO, or RESERVING A LIFE ESTATE to the decedent, then the Grantee(s) now own the property. For example, suppose the granting paragraph of the deed reads:

> PETER REILLY, a single man,
> party of the first part, and
> ROSE SMITH, a married woman,
> party of the second part
>
> RESERVING A LIFE ESTATE TO PETER REILLY,
>
> . . .

Peter Reilly is the owner of the life estate. While he is alive, the Grantee (Rose Smith) has no right to occupy the property. Once Peter dies, Rose owns the property, and is free to take possession of the property or transfer it, as she sees fit. As with a Joint Tenancy, nothing need be done to establish Rose's ownership of the property, however she should keep a certified copy of the death certificate in the event that she later decides to sell or transfer the property. Whoever does the closing will want to have proof that Rose is now the sole owner of the property.

DEED HELD AS HUSBAND AND WIFE

If a married couple hold property as follows:

TODD AMES AND SUSAN AMES, TENANTS BY THE ENTIRETIES

then when one spouse dies, and providing they are married at the time of death, the surviving spouse owns the property 100%. Maryland courts have ruled that property transferred to a husband and wife, for example,

TODD AMES AND SUSAN AMES, his wife - or -

TODD AMES AND SUSAN AMES, husband and wife

creates a Tenancy by the Entirety (*M. Lit, Inc. v. Berger*, 225 Md. 241 (1961), 170 A.2d 303).

As with a Joint Tenancy, ownership by the surviving spouse is automatic, however the decedent's name remains on the deed. The surviving spouse should keep a certified copy of the death certificate in the event that the spouse later decides to sell or transfer the property.

LAWYER DIVORCED PRIOR TO DEATH

If the decedent was divorced before he died, the Final Judgment should state who owns property held by the couple as Tenants By The Entireties (Family Law 8-202). If the deed to property owned by the couple has not been transferred to the proper owner, then you will need to consult with an attorney to have a new deed prepared and recorded that identifies the new owners of the property.

DEED HELD AS TENANTS IN COMMON

If the Grantee of a deed identifies the decedent and another as TENANTS IN COMMON then the decedent's share belongs to whomever the decedent named as his beneficiary in his Will. If the decedent died without a Will, then the Maryland Laws of Intestate Succession determine who inherits the property. See page 109 for an explanation of the law.

If a deed names two or more people as Grantees, but does not specifically state that they hold the property "AS JOINT TENANTS" or "IN JOINT TENANCY," then under Maryland law, they hold title as Tenants in

LAWYER — THE AMBIGUOUS DEED

Most deeds clearly state whether there are rights of survivorship. But some deeds can be read two ways. For example, suppose a woman deeds her home to herself and her two children as follows:

" . . . Ruth White party of the first part and
Ruth White, jointly with Ralph White and Susan Peters,
parties of the second part . . ."

Did Ruth intend that they all be joint tenants? Or did she intend that if one of her children died first, then that child's share would go to the deceased child's estate? Under Maryland law, they all could be holding the property as Tenants in Common, because the term "Joint Tenant" was not used. In such case, it may be necessary to have a Court decide who owns the property in the event that any of them die. It is important to consult with an attorney if you have any question about how to interpret the deed.

☎ **LAWYER** OUT OF STATE PROPERTY

The inheritance of real property located in the state of Maryland is determined by the laws of Maryland, and this is so regardless of whether the decedent was a resident of the state of Maryland. The laws of each state are similar, but not the same. For example the state of Massachuetts does not recognize a Tenancy By The Entirety. Married people in that state hold real property as Tenants-In-Common, unless the deed specifically states that there are righs of survivorship.

If the decedent owned property in another state, it is important to consult with an attorney in that state to determine who owns the property now that the Grantee is dead.

CAUTION THERE MAY BE A LATER DEED

This discussion on the different types of ownership of real property presumes that you are in possession of the most recent, valid deed. The decedent could have signed another, later, deed. Before you come to a conclusion about who inherits the property it is advisable to have an attorney or a title company do a title search to determine the owner of the property as of the decedent's date of death.

BANK/ SECURITY ACCOUNTS

If a bank account or security account is registered in the name of the decedent held "in trust for" or "for the benefit of" someone, then once the bank has a certified copy of the death certificate, the bank will turn over the account to the beneficiary (Finan. Instit. 1-204).

If the bank or security account is registered in the name of the decedent "as Trustee under a Trust agreement," that means the decedent was the Trustee of a Trust and the bank will turn over that account to the Successor Trustee of the Trust. Banks usually require a copy of the Trust agreement when the account was opened, so the bank probably knows the identity of the Successor Trustee. If the Trust was amended to name a different Successor Trustee, you need to present the bank with a copy of that amendment together with a certified copy of the death certificate.

MOTOR VEHICLE

If the motor vehicle is held in the name of the decedent "as Trustee," then the motor vehicle continues to be Trust property. The Successor Trustee will need to contact the motor vehicle bureau to have the title changed to that of the Successor Trustee. If the Trust agreement directs the Successor Trustee to sell the car or to distribute that car to a beneficiary, then the Successor Trustee will need to arrange to have this done. See Chapter 6 for directions about how to transfer the car to a new owner.

REAL PROPERTY

If the decedent had a Trust and put property that he owned into the Trust, then the deed may read something like this:

> This deed made the 14th day of August, 2000
> between JOHN ZAMORA
> and MARIA ZAMORA, GRANTOR
> and
> JOHN ZAMORA, **Trustee of the**
> **JOHN ZAMORA TRUST AGREEMENT**
> DATED FEBRUARY 26, 2000, GRANTEE
> . . .

The death of the Trustee of a Trust does not change the ownership of the property. It remains in the Trust. The Trust document might say whether the person who takes John's place as Trustee (the Successor Trustee) should sell or keep the property or perhaps give it to a beneficiary. If no instruction is given, the Successor Trustee can use his discretion as to what to do with the property. If you are a beneficiary of the Trust and you are concerned about what the Successor Trustee will do with the property, then it is best to consult with your attorney to learn about your rights under that Trust.

THE DEED OF TRUST

A Deed of Trust is very different from the above described deed. The Deed of Trust is essentially a mortgage. The owner of the property places title to the property with a Trustee as security for payment of monies owed to the lender. If the debt is not paid, then the Trustee (after proper foreclosure on the property) will deliver title to the property to the Beneficiary of the Deed of Trust, namely the lender (Real Prop. 7-101).

If the decedent owned property that was in his name only (not jointly with rights of survivorship, or in trust for someone), then some sort of Probate procedure will be necessary before the heirs can get possession of that property. Who is entitled to the decedent's Probate Estate depends on whether the decedent died ***testate*** (with a Will) or ***intestate*** (without a valid Will). If the decedent had a valid Will, then the beneficiaries of the decedent's property are identified in the Will.

If the decedent died without a Will, then the state of Maryland provides one for him in the form of a set of Laws of Intestate Succession. These laws determine who inherits the decedent's intestate Probate Estate and what percentage of the Probate Estate each heir is to receive once all the bills and costs of administering the Probate procedure are paid.

The law recognizes the right of the family to inherit the decedent's property. The law covers all possible relationships beginning with the decedent's spouse.

Who's The Spouse?

In this era of people challenging the concept of the family unit, those of a philosophical bent may ponder the meaning of marriage. Is it a union of two people in the eyes of God? Is it even a union? Maybe it is just a contract between two people. The state of Maryland does not concern itself with such things. If a person dies without a Will, then the state will distribute his property according to the laws of Maryland; and the laws of Maryland determine whether two people are married.

MARRIED IN MARYLAND

To be married in Maryland means that a man and a woman have obtained a license to marry from the Clerk of the Circuit Court, solemnized the marriage by a state or religious ceremony, and then lived together as man and wife. No one under the age of 15 may marry in the state of Maryland, and there are restrictions on the marriage of those between the ages of 15 and 17. The minor will either need the consent of a parent or guardian, or a physician must certify that the woman is pregnant, or has given birth to a child (Family Law 2-301).

THE COMMON LAW MARRIAGE

A common law marriage is one that has not been solemnized by ceremony. The couple agree to live together as man and wife, and then publicly hold themselves out as being married. Maryland does not recognize this as being a valid marriage, however Maryland courts have ruled that if the couple had a common law marriage in a state that recognizes such marriages, then Maryland will respect the laws of that state and recognize that marriage as being valid in the state of Maryland (*Jennings v. Jennings*, 20 Md. App. 369 (1974), 315 A.2d 816)

THE SAME SEX MARRIAGE

Vermont is the first, and as of this writing, the only, state to recognize same sex marriages, which they refer to as a "civil union." Several other states have passed statutes, specifically denying marital status to couples of the same gender regardless of whether that marriage is valid in any other state or country. The Maryland statute reads "Only a marriage between a man and a woman is valid in this State" (Family Law 2-201).

MARRIAGES PROHIBITED UNDER MARYLAND LAW

Bigamy is against the law in Maryland. It is punishable by imprisonment up to 9 years. In Maryland, it is also against the law for a man to marry his mother, sister, daughter, grandmother or granddaughter. A woman may not marry her father, brother, son, grandson, or grandfather (MC 27-18). Anyone who violates this law is guilty of a misdemeanor and is subject to a fine of $1,500 or to permanent banishment from the state of Maryland.

In addition, a man may not marry his aunt, niece, stepmother, stepdaughter, mother-in-law, grandmother-in-law, daughter-in-law or granddaughter-in-law. A woman may not marry her uncle, nephew, stepfather, stepson, father-in-law, grandfather-in-law, son-in-law or grandson-in-law (Family Law 2-202). Anyone who violates this law is guilty of a misdemeanor and is subject to a fine of $500.

All of the above marriages are ***void***, meaning that the marriage is not legal in the state of Maryland. Anyone can challenge such marriage as being invalid. For example, suppose the decedent married his daughter-in-law (after she divorced his son, of course). If the decedent made a Will leaving all of his property to his wife, then she would have the right to that property, because the decedent was free to leave his property to anyone he wished. But if he died without a Will, someone (no doubt the son) could challenge her right to inherit under the Maryland Laws of Intestate Succession. If the challenge were successful, the marriage would be declared to be void, and the wife would receive nothing.

If you have any question about the validity of the decedent's marriage, then it is important to consult with an attorney.

If the decedent neglected to make a Will, then the state of Maryland provides one for him in the Maryland Laws of Intestate Succession. The Law provides for the distribution of the ***Net Estate***, i.e. whatever is left after payment of all valid debts and taxes, but not including the Maryland Inheritance Tax which is paid for by the person who actually inherits the property (see page 36).

✧ MARRIED, NO CHILD, NO PARENT

The ***surviving spouse*** is one whose marriage to the decedent was valid in the state of Maryland and who did not commit bigamy while married to the decedent, and who did not divorce or annul their marriage, in this or any other state prior to the death (Est. & Trusts 1-202). The surviving spouse inherits the entire Net Probate Estate provided the decedent had no surviving ***lineal descendant*** (child, grandchild, great-grandchild, etc.), and no surviving parent.

✧ MARRIED, NO CHILD, SURVIVING PARENT

If decedent was married and had no surviving lineal descendant, but he had a surviving parent, then the spouse gets the first $15,000 and half of whatever is left. The parent gets the other half. If both parents survive the decedent then they share that half equally.

✧ MARRIED, WITH DESCENDANTS

If the decedent was married and with a minor child, the spouse takes half and the child the other half of the Net Probate Estate. If there is no minor child, but one or more lineal descendants, then the spouse takes the first $15,000, plus half of whatever is left. The decedent's lineal descendants inherit the other half (Est. & Trusts 3-102).

✧ CHILD, NO SPOUSE

If the decedent was single, then his children inherit the Net Estate, ***by representation***, meaning that if all the children are alive, they each take an equal share of the Net Estate; but if one child dies before the decedent, then the share intended for the deceased child is given to the his/her children, in equal shares. If the deceased child died without lineal descendants, then the surviving children divide the Net Estate equally between them (Est. & Trusts 1-210, 3-103).

✧ NO CHILD, NO SPOUSE

If the decedent had no spouse or lineal descendant, then his property is divided equally between his parents. If only one of his parents is alive, then all of the property goes to that parent. If neither parent is alive, then the estate goes to the decedent's brothers and sisters, by representation. No distinction is made between relatives of half blood; in particular, a sibling with the same set of parents as the decedent, inherits the same as a sibling who shares only one parent with the decedent (Est. & Trusts 1-204)

If the decedent had no brothers, sisters, nephews or nieces, great-nieces, great-nephews, etc., then the Net Estate is divided with half going to the decedent's grandparents (or to the survivor) on his mother's side. If neither maternal grandparent is alive, the property goes to their lineal descendants by representation. If there are no lineal descendants, then the entire Net Estate goes to the paternal grandparents (or their lineal descendants), by representation.

The other half is distributed in the same manner; i.e., half goes to the decedent's grandparents (or to the survivor) father's side. Again, if neither paternal grandparent is alive, then to their lineal descendants, by representation. If there are no surviving lineal descendants, then the entire Net Estate goes to the maternal grandparents, or their lineal descendants, by representation.

NO BLOOD RELATIVES BUT SURVIVING STEPCHILDREN

If a person dies without a Will and he has absolutely no surviving blood relatives, but does have surviving stepchildren (or their lineal descendants), then the stepchildren inherit the Net Estate, by representation (Est. & Trusts 3-104).

THE STATE: HEIR OF LAST RESORT

If the decedent did not leave a Will, and no blood relative, nor stepchild can be found, then the money goes to the state of Maryland. If the decedent was receiving long term care benefits under Maryland's Medical Assistance Program at the time of his death, then the entire Net Estate goes to the Maryland Department of Health and Mental Hygiene. If he was not receiving medical assistance, then the Net Estate goes to the Board of Education in the county where the Letters were granted.

If it later happens that a blood relative learns of the death, he or she can make a claim for the money. If the claim is granted, then the Net Estate (without interest) will be given to the relative (Est. & Trusts 3-105).

CAUTION IT ISN'T ALL THAT SIMPLE

The explanation in this book of the Laws of Intestate Succession is abridged. Even though you may now know more about the Maryland's Laws of Intestate Succession than you ever wanted to know, there is much more to the law. For example, we did not explain in detail exactly how the estate is distributed if the decedent is survived only by descendants of his maternal or paternal grandparents. We could give an example explaining the law, but we thought you might enjoy a puzzle instead:

Winston died intestate leaving $100,000. His only relatives were his Aunt Susie (on his mother's side) and her two children Ramona and Abigail, and a second cousin Elvis (i.e., the son of a deceased cousin), on his father's side. How much does each relative receive?

You can check your answer by visiting the Maryland section of the Eagle Publishing Company Web site:

http://www.eaglepublishing.com

WHO DIED FIRST?

Maryland statute requires that an heir survive the decedent by at least 30 days in order to inherit property according to the Maryland's Laws of Intestate Succession. If an heir does not live for at least 30 days after the decedent's death, then the decedent's property is distributed as if the heir died first. This rule also applies to property inherited by Will, unless the Will makes some different provision. This rule does not apply to the decedent's spouse; i.e., if the spouse dies within 30 days of the death of the decedent, then the surviving spouse (or the Estate of the surviving spouse) is entitled to inherit the decedent's property in the same way as if the surviving spouse had lived for at least 30 days (Est. & Trusts 3-110, 4-401; Courts & Jud. Proc. 10-805).

Sometimes it happens that two family members die simultaneously, and no one know who died first. For example, suppose a father and son die together in a car crash, how is the property distributed in that case?

Maryland statute provides for an orderly distribution of their respective estates. Each person is assumed to have survived the other and the property of each is distributed on that basis. The father's property is distributed as if he survived his son and the son's property is distributed as if he survived his father. For example, if the father had a $10,000 insurance policy with his son as beneficiary and his daughter as alternate beneficiary, then the money will go to his daughter (Courts & Jud. Proc. 10-804).

If the father and son owned property jointly and they die simultaneously, the property is divided with one half going to the estate of the father and the other half to the estate of his son. (Courts & Jud. Proc. 10-803).

THE RIGHTS OF A CHILD

ADOPTED CHILD An adopted child has the same rights to inherit property from his adoptive parents as does a natural child. Upon adoption, the adoptive child has no right to inherit property from his natural parents unless the child is adopted by the spouse of the child's natural parent (Est. & Trusts 1-205, 1-207).

AFTERBORN CHILD If the decedent's child was conceived prior to the decedent's death, and born after the death, then the child inherits the same as any other child of the decedent. This does not apply to any other relationship. For example, if a grandchild is conceived prior to the death, but not born until after the death, that grandchild does not inherit under Maryland's Laws of Intestate Succession (Est. & Trusts 3-107).

NON-MARITAL CHILD

A child born out of wedlock has the same rights to inherit from his/her natural father as does one born in wedlock, provided:

- ☑ the decedent participated in a marriage ceremony with the child's mother before the birth regardless of whether the attempted marriage was valid - or -
- ☑ the decedent openly acknowledged the child as his own and his paternity was commonly known - or -
- ☑ the decedent participated in a marriage ceremony with the child's mother after the birth and acknowledged that he was the father of the child - or -
- ☑ the decedent signed a document acknowledging that the child is his - or -
- ☑ his paternity was established by a court.

(Est. & Trusts 1-206, 1-208)

If the decedent denied his paternity, then it will take a court procedure to establish (or disprove) paternity.

Medical technology has made important contributions to solving the problem of infertility. There are all sorts of solutions, from hormone replacement therapy, to sperm banks that provide donations anonymously, to frozen sperm and/or ova to be thawed and used at a later date, to women who are a surrogate or gestational mother, and not the biological parent of the child.

Solving a set of medical problems has opened the door to a new set of legal problems. Used to be, the only question was "Who's the father?" Now it could well be "Who's the mother? Two major problems are the case of a woman who has an assisted conception without the knowledge and/or consent of her spouse; and the case of a child born to a surrogate mother.

Under Maryland law, if a child is born to parents using any form of assisted conception, including artificial insemination, then that child has the same rights as a child born the old fashioned way. It is presumed that the spouse of a woman who is artificially inseminated consented to the procedure (Est. & Trusts 1-206). If that is not the case, then the father can take legal steps to sever his rights and responsibilities as a parent.

As of this writing, there is no Maryland statute dealing with the children born to surrogate parents. Other states have taken various positions from Michigan where surrogate parenting contracts are strictly prohibited, to Virginia the court supervises the surrogate contract and then issues a birth certificate to the intended parents after the birth. In Maryland, a child born to a surrogate mother is the child of the mother, unless adopted by the intended parents. And this is so, regardless of whether either intended parent happens to be the biological parent of the child.

☎ LAWYER THE "FORGOTTEN CHILD"

We discussed the rights of children when the parent dies without a Will, but suppose the decedent left a Will and did not include anything for a child. Is that child entitled to some part of the decedent's estate? The answer is "no," provided the decedent left a valid Will clearly stating that it was the decedent's wish not to give anything to the child (Est. & Trusts 3-301).

But suppose, the decedent made no mention of the child. Suppose, he simply "forgot" to include something for that child or perhaps he made the Will before the child was born. In such case, the child could challenge the Will arguing that the decedent simply "forgot" to include something for that child. Such challenge will probably provoke a court battle. The named beneficiaries, will no doubt argue that the decedent was estranged from the forgotten" child, and that the omission was deliberate.

If you wish to challenge a Will on this, or any other ground, you can expect a court battle. You will need to employ an attorney experienced in litigation matters to do so.

READING THE WILL

If the decedent left a Will, then the Will states who is to receive the property. Most Wills are short and easy to read, however, you may come across a Will that did not make provision for what would happen to a gift in the event the intended beneficiary of the gift dies first. In such case, Maryland law provides that the gift be distributed as if the person owned the property before he died. For example, suppose the decedent's Will gives a gift of $10,000 to his brother, and did not name an alternate beneficiary of the gift. If the decedent's brother died after the Will was written, but before the death of the Will maker, then the $10,000 will be distributed according to the brother's Will. If the brother died without a Will, then the $10,000 is distributed according to Maryland's Laws of Intestate Succession as part of the brother's Net Estate (Est. & Trusts 4-403).

It could happen that the decedent left a gift to a group of people and did not make provision for how the gift was to be distributed in the event that a member of the group died first. In such case Maryland statute (Est. & Trusts 1-210.1) determines how the property is to be distributed. The statute is fairly complex, so it is best to consult with an attorney in such event.

THE TERROR CLAUSE

Some Wills contain a provision known as an "In Terrorem Clause" which is Latin for "in terror or warning paragraph." It is a provision in the Will that says, in effect, that anyone who challenges the Will is disinherited. Some states allow such provisions, but in Maryland, if someone challenges a Will, and that challenge is reasonable in light of all the circumstances, then the clause has no legal effect and the Will is read as if the clause did not exist (Est. & Trusts 4-413).

WHEN TO CHALLENGE THE WILL

It is not uncommon for a family member to be unhappy with the way the decedent willed his property. If you are tempted to challenge a Will, first consider whether the Will is valid under Maryland law.

In Maryland, a Will is presumed to be valid if at the time the decedent made the Will:

- he was at least 18 years of age
- he was legally competent to make a Will (Est. & Trusts 4-101).

Unless the decedent had, prior to executing the Will, been found by a Court to lack legal capacity, it is presumed that the decedent was legally competent to make a Will. Maryland courts have ruled that anyone challenging the Will has the difficult task of proving that such was not the case. To challenge the decedent's capacity, you need to prove he did not know what he was doing (namely making a Will), nor did he know what property he had, or even how he wanted to dispose of his property, and that he did not remember or understand his relationship to his family (*Slicer v. Griffith*, 27 Md. App. 502 (1975), 341 A.2d 838).

Many times the Will maker is legally competent, but has diminished (reduced) capacity and is pressured into preparing his Will a certain way. In such cases you may be able to prove that there was ***undue influence*** and that the decedent was not acting intelligently, or voluntarily, but rather according to the will of someone who dominated the decedent. Of course, for any given set of circumstances you need to consult with an attorney experienced in Probate litigation to learn of options that may be available to you.

THE UNWITNESSED WILL

The first step in the Probate procedure is to have the Probate court determine whether the Will presented is valid. If the Will is in writing and signed by the Will maker in the presence of at least two credible witnesses, then there should be no problem in having the Will accepted into Probate. If the Will is notarized, then the Court will probably not require further proof. If the Will is witnessed but not notarized, then the court will ask the witnesses to testify that they saw the Will maker sign the Will.

But suppose the decedent wrote out a Will in his own hand and signed it with no one present? Such a Will is called a ***holographic Will.*** Many states (including Maryland) refuse to accept a holographic Will into Probate. The problem with a holographic Will, in this or any other state, is its authenticity. Because no one saw the decedent sign the Will, it is hard to determine whether the Will was written by the decedent or is a forgery.

AN EXCEPTION TO THE RULE

Maryland statute does allow a holographic Will to be admitted to Probate if the decedent was a member of the armed services of the United States and made the Will while he was outside of U.S. territory. But the Will is not valid if the decedent had been discharged from the service for more than a year (Est. & Trusts 4-103).

Regardless of whether the decedent was a member of the armed services, if all the decedent left was a holographic Will, you need to consult with an attorney experienced in Probate matters, to present evidence to the Court that the Will does (or does not) qualify as a holographic Will in the state of Maryland.

THE VERBAL WILL

Picture a death bed scene. The elderly gentleman is surrounded by several family members. In a whisper, just audible enough to be heard, he says:

"Even though I am a wealthy man, I never got around to making a Will. You all have been good to me, but I did want my entire fortune to go to my nephew, Robert. He has been like a son to me. "

Do you think Robert can inherit his Uncle's estate?

Not in Maryland unless:

⇨ Someone writes down his uncle's wishes, and
⇨ The uncle acknowledges that this is his Will, and
⇨ The uncle tells someone to sign the Will for him, and
⇨ The person does so, and two people sign the Will as witnesses (Est. & Trusts 4-102).

Considering that the uncle's relatives will probably inherit the fortune under the Maryland Laws of Intestate Succession, it is doubtful that Robert is in danger of becoming wealthy at any time in the near future.

THE WILL THAT IS CONTRARY TO LAW

Sometimes a person who is of sound mind, makes a Will, but that Will has the effect of giving a spouse less than the spouse is entitled to receive under Maryland law. One such example is that of Nancy. Hers was not an easy life. She divorced her hard drinking first husband. The final judgment gave her their homestead, some securities and sole custody of their daughter. Some years later Nancy met and married Harry. Nancy wanted to be sure to provide for her daughter so she wrote out a Will giving her car and household furnishings to Harry and everything else to her daughter. The following year she gave birth to a son, but did not change her Will.

Nancy's son was 5 and her daughter 19, when Nancy died after a lengthy battle with cancer. Just before she died, Nancy gave $20,000 to her daughter to see her through the first year of college. She also spoke about her Will "My Will leaves everything to you. I didn't bother to change it because your stepfather has a good job, and he is a good father, so I know he and your brother will do just fine."

Nancy did not have much when she died — the house, her household furnishings and some personal items. Her securities and bank accounts were worth about $50,000.

When the funeral was over, Harry discovered the Will (leaving all to his stepdaughter). He also found the cancelled $20,000 check, but the thing that made him ballistic, was having his stepdaughter tell him that she was putting the house up for sale, and he would have to move out.

Harry went to his attorney.

"I was a good husband to Nancy, supporting and taking care of her all during her illness. It was me, and not her daughter, who was at her side when she died. Don't I have any rights? And what about my son? Doesn't he have any rights?"

"Your son was born after Nancy made her Will. Under Maryland statute (Est. & Trusts 3-301) he is entitled to as he would have received if your wife died without a Will. You also have many rights provided you did not give up those rights. Maryland statute (Est. & Trusts 3-205) allows you to ***waive*** (give up) you rights by signing an agreement such as a prenuptial or postnuptial agreement. Did you sign any such document?"

"Absolutely not!"

"In that case, under Maryland statute, you are entitled to an ***Elective Share*** of her estate, which is one-third of her estate. If your wife had no children, you would have been entitled to half her estate (Est. & Trusts 3-203). In addition, you are entitled to a Family Allowance of $5,000, and your son is entitled to a Family Allowance of $2,500. Your stepdaughter is over 18 so she is not entitled to an allowance (Est. & Trusts 3-201).

Harry was still upset "But her house is worth the most amount of money. Don't I have Dower rights or something?"

"Dower rights are for widows. Curtesy rights are for widowers. But in Maryland those rights were abolished long before you were married (Est. & Trusts 3-202). But you still are entitled to 1/3rd the value of the house as part of your Elective Share. Your son is entitled to the same inheritance as he would have received if she died without a Will. If Nancy died without a Will you would have receive half her estate and the children would have shared the other half, so your son would is entitled to 25% of her Net Probate Estate (Est. & Trusts 3-102). With your 1/3rd Elective Share and his 1/4th intestate share, together you will own 7/12ths or over 58% of the house."

Harry said "And what about the $20,000 she gave to her daughter just before she died?"

"That does not get counted as part of her inheritance unless your wife amended her Will, or left some other document saying she wanted the monies subtracted or unless your stepdaughter agrees to accept $20,000 less."

"No chance that will happen."

The attorney said "The Court will decide who is entitled to what. The Elective Share is not automatic. The Court will hold a hearing and determine whether you have a right to that money. Your stepdaughter will have an opportunity to voice any objection she may have. If the Court determines that you are entitled to the money, then the court will decide how it is to be paid. You will need to sign a ***petition*** (a request), which I will prepare, requesting your Elective Share. I will file it in the Probate Court. This must be done within 7 months of the filing of the Will or the appointment of a Personal Representative, whichever date is later" (Est. & Trusts 3-206).

Nancy's daughter did not fare as well as her mother intended. There was no cash left in the estate after the funeral expenses, medical bills, costs of administration and family allowance were paid. All the daughter inherited was her 1/3rd share of the house, and she didn't get that until it was sold the following year.

No doubt Nancy did not understand what would happen to her estate once she passed on. The Will she left did not accomplish her goal of providing for her daughter. All it did was cause turmoil and an irreparable rift within the family. It didn't need to be that way. Had Nancy known about Maryland law, she could have consulted with an attorney and set up an estate plan that could have provided for her daughter, without alienating her husband and son.

But, the moral of the story, for the purpose of this discussion, is that if you believe that the decedent's Will is not valid or is not drafted according to Maryland law, then you need to consult with an attorney experienced in Probate matters to determine your legal rights under that Will.

Getting Possession Of The Property 6

Knowing who is entitled to receive the decedent's property is one thing. Getting that property is another. As explained in the previous chapter if the decedent held property jointly with someone, or in a trust for someone, the property now belongs to the joint owner or beneficiary. If it is personal property such as a bank account or a security, the beneficiary can usually get possession of the property by giving a certified copy of the death certificate to the financial institution.

If the decedent had real or personal property in his name only, or if he held property as a Tenant-In-Common, then upon his death, the Personal Representative has legal title to that property (Est. & Trusts 1-301). A Probate procedure is necessary in order to transfer title from the Personal Representative to the proper beneficiary. In most cases a Regular Probate procedure is necessary that may require the assistance of an attorney; but there are two shortened Probate procedures that can be done without legal assistance, namely the ***Small Estate Administration*** and the ***Modified Administration.*** In this chapter, we will discuss these methods of transferring the decedent's property to the proper beneficiary.

Too often, the first person to discover the body will help himself to the decedent's ***personal property*** (clothing, jewelry, appliances, electrical equipment, cameras, books, household items and furnishing, etc.). Unless that person is the decedent's sole beneficiary, such action is unconscionable, if not illegal.

If the decedent was married, then personal property that they owned jointly now belongs to the surviving spouse. Separate property owned by the decedent becomes part of his Probate Estate to be distributed by the Personal Representative.

If the decedent was not married, then all his personal effects should be given to the person appointed as the Personal Representative. The Representative has the duty to distribute the property according to the decedent's Will, or according to Maryland's Laws of Intestate Succession in the event he died without a Will.

If you determine that there is no need for a Probate procedure and the decedent did not have a Will then his next of kin need to divide all of the personal effects among themselves in approximately equal proportions.

What's Equal?

The decedent's Will or if no Will, then the Maryland Laws of Intestate Succession may direct that the decedent's personal property be divided equally between two or more beneficiaries. The problem with the term "equal" is that people have different ideas of what "equal" means. Unless there is clear evidence that the decedent's Will meant something else, "equal" refers to the monetary value of the item and not to the number of items received.

For example, to divide the decedent's personal effects equally, one beneficiary may receive an expensive item of jewelry and another beneficiary may receive several items whose overall value is approximately equal to that single piece of jewelry.

When distributing personal effects there needs to be cooperation and perhaps compromise, or else bitter arguments might arise over items of little monetary value. One such argument occurred when an elderly woman died who was rich only in her love for her five children and 12 grandchildren. After the funeral, the children gathered in their mother's apartment. Each child had his/her own furnishings and no need for anything in the apartment. They agreed to donate all of their mother's personal effects to a local charity with the exception of a few items of sentimental value.

Each child took some small item as a remembrance — a handkerchief, a large platter that their mother used to serve family dinners, a doily their mother crocheted. Things went smoothly until it came to her photograph album. Frank, the youngest sibling, said, "I'll take this." Marie objected saying, "But there are pictures in that album that I want."

Frank retorted, "You already took all the pictures Mom had on her dresser." The argument went downhill from there. Unsettled sibling rivalries boiled over, fueled by the hurt of the loss that they were all experiencing.

It almost came to blows when the eldest settled the argument: "Frank you make copies of all of the photos in the album for Marie. Marie, you make copies of all of the pictures that you took and give them to Frank. This way you both will have a complete set of Mom's pictures. And while you're at it, make copies for the rest of us."

TRANSFERRING THE CAR

As explained on Page 98, if the decedent owned a car jointly with his spouse, then the surviving spouse now owns the car 100%. All the spouse need do is to go to the nearest full service branch of the Motor Vehicle Administration to transfer title to the car. In all other cases, a Personal Representative will need to be appointed in order to transfer the car to the proper beneficiary. If the decedent had a Will and he made a specific gift of the car to someone, the Personal Representative will transfer the car to that person. If there was no mention of the car in his Will, then the car goes to the ***residuary beneficiaries*** under the Will, i.e., those who inherit whatever is left once all the bills have been paid and all the special gifts made in the Will are distributed.

If the decedent did not have a Will, then the car goes to the decedent's heirs as determined by the Maryland's Laws of Intestate Succession (see page 109).

You may want to limit the use of the car until it is transferred to the beneficiary. If the decedent's car is involved in an accident before the car is transferred to the new owner, then the decedent's estate may be liable for the damage. Having adequate insurance on the car may save the estate from monetary loss, but a pending lawsuit could delay Probate and prevent any money from being distributed to the beneficiaries until the lawsuit is settled.

TRANSFER WHEN MORE THAN ONE BENEFICIARY

If there is more than one person who has the right to inherit the car, then they all can take title to the car. That may not be a practical thing to do since only one person can drive the car at any given time and if one gets into an accident, then they all can be held liable. The better route is for the beneficiaries to agree to have one person take title to the car. The person taking title will need to compensate the others for their share of the car. In such case the beneficiaries need to come to an agreement as to the value of the car.

DETERMINING THE VALUE OF THE CAR

Cars are valued in many different ways. The ***collateral*** value of the car is the value that banks use to evaluate the car for purposes of making a loan to the owner of the car. Because banks print these values in book form, the collateral value is also referred to as the ***book value*** of the car. If you were to trade in a car for the purpose of purchasing a new car, then the car dealer will offer you the ***wholesale*** value of the car. Were you to purchase that same car from a car dealer, then he will price it at its ***retail*** or ***fair market value***. Usually the retail price is highest, wholesale is lowest and the book value of the car is somewhere in between.

You can call your local bank to get the book value of the car. It may be more difficult to obtain the wholesale value of the car because the amount of money a dealer is willing to pay for the car depends on the value of the new car that you are purchasing. You can determine the car's retail value by looking at comparable used car advertisements in the local newspaper or over the Internet.

It is the Personal Representative's job to transfer the motor vehicle to the proper beneficiary. He can do so anytime after he receives his Letters authorizing him to administer the estate. If there could be a creditor problem, he may decide not to make any transfers until 6 months have passed and all the claims have been filed against the estate.

If you are the beneficiary of the car, you might want to go with the Personal Representative to the MVA and transfer the car registration at the same time that he transfers title to the car. You will need to obtain insurance on the car and a Certificate of Inspection before taking title to the car. You may want to first call to determine what information will be required. Their in-state toll-free number is (800) 950-1682. Out of state call (301) 729-4550; or visit their Web site:

MARYLAND MOTOR VEHICLE ADMINISTRATION
http://www.mva.state.md.us/

If the car is going to be transferred out of state, then the Personal Representative needs to cancel the Maryland registration. He should also cancel the decedent's driver's license at the same time and have the decedent's name deleted from the MVA mailing list.

TRANSFERRING THE MOBILE HOME

Mobile homes that do not exceed 35' in length need to be titled and registered with the Motor Vehicle Administration ("MVA"). Transfers are made in the same manner as a motor vehicle. You need to go to the nearest full service branch Office with a certified copy of the death certificate. You may want to first call and ask what other information they may require.

Before transferring the mobile home, you need to find out whether the land on which the mobile home is located was leased or owned by the decedent. If the decedent was renting space in a trailer park, then you need to contact the trailer park owner to transfer the lease agreement to the beneficiary of the mobile home. If the decedent owned the land under the mobile home, then a Probate procedure will be necessary to transfer the land to the proper beneficiary. See page 135 for information about transferring real property.

TRANSFERRING THE BOAT

The Personal Representative will need to go to the Department of Natural Resources ("DNR") to transfer title and registration of the decedent's motor boat. There are some 350 DNR Service Centers located throughout Maryland. You can call the DNR at (410) 260-8200 for the Service Center nearest you, or you visit their Web site:

MARYLAND DEPARTMENT OF NATURAL RESOURCES
http://www.dnr.state.md.us/

Special Situation

TRANSFERRING THE LEASED CAR

The leased car is not an asset of the estate because the decedent did not own the car. The leased car is a liability to the estate because the decedent was obligated to pay the balance of the monies owed on the lease agreement. The Personal Representative, or next of kin, needs to work out an agreement with the company to either assign the lease to a beneficiary or family member who will agree to pay for the lease — or to have the estate pay off the lease by purchasing the car under the terms of the lease agreement.

Some lenders will allow the lease to be assigned to a beneficiary provided the estate remains liable for the balance of payment. In such case, it is better to have the beneficiary refinance the car and have the original lease agreement paid in full.

If the remaining payments exceed the current market value of the car, there may be a temptation to hand the keys over to the leasing company. This may not be the best strategy, because the leasing company can sell the car and then sue the estate for the balance of the monies owed. If the decedent had no assets, then simply returning the car may be an option. But if the decedent's estate has assets available to pay the balance of the lease payments, then the Personal Representative needs to arrange to have the car transferred in a way that releases the estate from all further liability.

INCOME TAX REFUNDS

Any refund due to the decedent under a joint federal income tax return filed by his surviving spouse will be sent to the surviving spouse. If the decedent's Personal Representative filed the final return, then the refund check will be sent to him to be deposited to the estate account.

If the decedent was single and no Probate procedure is necessary, then whoever is entitled to decedent's estate is entitled to the refund check. If you are the beneficiary of the decedent's estate, you can obtain the refund by filing IRS form 1310 along with the decedent's final income tax return (the 1040). You can obtain form 1310 from the decedent's accountant, or if he did not have an accountant and you wish to file yourself, you can call the IRS at (800) 829-3676 to obtain the form. You can get instructions, publications and forms from the Internal Revenue Service Web site:

IRS WEB SITE
IRS FORMS AND INSTRUCTIONS
http://www.irs.ustreas.gov/prod/forms_pubs/forms.html
IRS PUBLICATIONS
http://www.irs.ustreas.gov/prod/forms_pubs/pubs.html

The Personal Representative does not need to file form 1310 because once he files the decedent's final income tax return, any refund will be forwarded to him. Similarly, it is not necessary for the surviving spouse who filed a joint return to file form 1310.

THE STATE INCOME TAX REFUND

The decedent's final Maryland State income tax return needs to be filed at the same time the federal income tax return is filed. As with the federal return, the surviving spouse can file a joint return, and any state income tax refund will be distributed to the spouse. If there is no surviving spouse, then the Personal Representative needs to file the final state income tax return.

You can get filing information and download forms from the Comptroller's Web site:

THE COMPTROLLER OF MARYLAND
http://www.comp.state.md.us/

Any refund will be sent to the Personal Representative to be deposited to the estate account. You can check the refund status by calling (800) 218-8160.

You may want to check the decedent's income tax return for the past 3 years to see whether he is entitled to a refund. See page 68 if you cannot locate his last 3 returns. There is a 3 year Statute of Limitations for filing a claim for an income tax refund, so there is no need to look back more than 3 years (Tax-Gen 13-1104).

No Probate procedure is necessary to transfer real property if the decedent held that property:

- ⇨ as the owner of a Life Estate — or —
- ⇨ jointly with Right of Survivorship — or —
- ⇨ with his spouse as Tenants-by-the-Entirety.

The property belongs to the surviving owner as of the date of death. Nothing need be done to establish that ownership, although the surviving owner should keep a certified copy of the death certificate to produce in the event that someone requests proof of ownership.

No Inheritance Tax need be paid on the transfer of the decedent's share of the property to the surviving owner, provided the surviving owner is the decedent's

- ~ spouse or stepchild
- ~ descendant (child, grandchild, etc.)
- ~ spouse of a descendant (son or daughter-in-law, etc.)
- ~ parent or stepparent or grandparent
- ~ brother or sister.

But if the surviving owner is a friend, cousin, nephew, niece, or anyone else not mentioned above, then the surviving owner must pay his share of the Inheritance Tax (Tax-Gen. 7-203). If there is a Probate procedure, the Personal Representative will have the surviving owner contribute his share of the Inheritance Tax. If no Probate procedure is necessary, then the surviving owner will need to file an Information Report with the Register of Wills and pay the Inheritance Tax at that time (Tax-Gen. 7-214).

☎ LAWYER

TRANSFERRING OUT OF STATE PROPERTY HELD JOINTLY

Each state regulates the transfer of real property within that state. Many states have rules much like Maryland, i.e., no document need be recorded to transfer real property to a joint tenant who has a right of survivorship, or to a remainder beneficiary of a Life Estate interest. It is the practice in some states, such as Ohio and Illinois to record an Affidavit that describes the transfer of the property to the surviving joint owner.

Some states, such as Florida, allow the death certificate to be recorded in the county where the property is located, so that anyone examining title to the property will know who now owns the property. In Florida, the Clerk of the Circuit Court is in charge of recording deeds and death certificates. You may want to call the recording department in the county where the property is located to find out what documents (if any) need to recorded to let people know of the death. The name of the official in charge of recording deeds varies state to state. In some states it is the County Registrar or the County Recorder or as mentioned, the Clerk of the Circuit Court.

Of course, if the decedent owned real property in his own name or as a Tenant In Common, you need to contact an attorney in that state to have the property transferred to the proper beneficiary.

If the decedent owned property in his name only, then a Probate procedure will be necessary regardless of whether he left 1 hundred dollars or 1 million dollars. There is a Small Estate Administration for estates that do not exceed $30,000 ($50,000 if the surviving spouse is the sole beneficiary) and a Modified Administration if the Personal Representative and/or the decedents spouse or children are the only beneficiaries of the estate. With the exception of accounting duties, the procedure for the Small Estate Administration and the Modified Administration are much the same as the Regular Probate Administration. In each case someone must go to Court and ask to be appointed as Personal Representative. Whoever is named in the Will to serve as Personal Representative has top priority. If that person cannot, or will not serve, then the surviving spouse has priority. If there is no surviving spouse, or if the spouse cannot or will not serve, then any of the residuary beneficiaries of the Will can serve as Personal Representative.

The order of priority for appointing a Personal Representative if there is no Will is as follows:

- 1st spouse and/or adult children of decedent
- 2nd grandchildren
- 3rd parents
- 4th Adult brothers and sisters
- 5th Any other relation
- 6th The decedent's largest creditor
- 7th Anyone else who has a monetary interest
- 8th Any other person (Est. & Trusts 5-104).

Who shall serve as Personal Representative is usually agreed upon by the family. In the event of a dispute, the Court will determine who is best suited for the job.

THE PETITION FOR PROBATE

Whoever volunteers to serve as Personal Representative must file a PETITION FOR PROBATE with the Register of Wills. The Petition is a request to the Court to be appointed as Personal Representative. The form of the Petition is set by Maryland Statute (Est. & Trusts 5-206). The form contains basic information:

- the date of death and decedent's residence;
- the reason you are entitled to serve as Personal Representative;
- the estimated value of the estate;
- who is entitled to inherit the estate.

The form of the Petition is the same regardless of the size of the estate. You can get the Petition For Probate (and all other statutory Probate forms) from the Register of Wills or you can download the forms from the Register's Web site:

MARYLAND REGISTER OF WILLS
http://www.registers.state.md.us

The Web site also lists the name, address and telephone numbers of all of the local Register of Wills.

Maryland's Attorney General together with the Register of Wills has put out a publication entitled:

ADMINISTERING ESTATES IN MARYLAND

This publication explains all of the things that need to be done to settle the decedent's estate. You can get the publication from the Register of Wills, or you can download it from the above Web site.

D.I.Y?

With all of the information available from the Internet and the Register of Wills available to assist, you may be wondering whether to "Do It Yourself" or employ an attorney to help you through the process. The answer depends on your individual circumstance. Certainly consider doing it yourself if all of the following apply:

MORE TIME THAN MONEY

If you are going to serve as Personal Representative, you will need to spend considerable time reading about how to administer the estate. And you will need to spend even more time preparing and filing the necessary forms. An attorney can save you time and effort, but the downside is the cost of his services. However, don't assume that the attorney's fees will be prohibitive. Many attorneys, who are experienced in Probate matters, offer a flat fee for their services. Before making a decision, it is worth a few calls to comparison shop. Once you know the going rate, you can determine whether you want to employ an attorney to help you through the process.

NO ANTICIPATED PROBLEM

You can risk personal liability if all of the valid claims are not properly paid (Est. & Trusts 8-109). If there is not enough money in the estate to pay all of the creditors, or if you expect that there may be a dispute as to monies owed by the decedent, then it is best to seek the counsel of an attorney.

You should also seek the counsel of an attorney if you anticipate any other problem such as a dispute about who is to serve as Personal Representative or whether the decedent left a valid Will, or whether someone is, or is not entitled to a share of the estate.

YOUR RIGHTS AS A BENEFICIARY

It is important that you, as a beneficiary of the decedent's estate, know what rights you have and where necessary, how to assert those rights.

✧ RIGHT TO YOUR OWN ATTORNEY

The attorney who handles the estate is employed by, and represents, the Personal Representative. If the estate is sizeable, then consider employing your own attorney to check that things are done properly and in a timely manner. Even with a small estate, you may want to consult with an attorney if at any time you are concerned about the way the Probate is being conducted.

✧ RIGHT TO APPROVE OF THE PERSONAL REPRESENTATIVE

Once a Personal Representative is appointed, the Register of Wills will have a NOTICE OF APPOINTMENT published in a local newspaper to let the decedent's creditors know of the death. The Register will mail you a copy of that Notice to let you know the identity of the Personal Representative. If you have an objection to the appointment, then you need to let the Court know of your objection as soon as you learn of the intended appointment (Est. & Trusts 2-102).

You have the right to go before the Court on your own, but before doing so, you should consult with a Probate attorney. An experienced attorney will know what arguments will sway the Court, and what arguments will fail. The attorney can explain the best way for you to present your concerns to the Court.

✧ RIGHT TO A COPY OF THE WILL

If there is a Will then you have the right to receive a copy of that Will. Once the Personal Representative is appointed have him or his attorney forward the copy to you. You have the right to challenge the validity of the Will at any time up to 6 months after the Personal Representative has been appointed (Est. & Trusts 5-207). For example, suppose a Will is submitted to Probate and you discover another later Will, then you can challenge the validity of the Will that was admitted to Probate. As discussed above, it is best to seek the counsel of an attorney to challenge the validity of a Will.

✧ RIGHT TO DEMAND SUFFICIENT BOND

It doesn't happen often, but every now and again a Personal Representative will run off with estate funds. A bond is insurance for the estate. If estate monies are stolen then the company that issued the bond will reimburse the estate for the loss. Most Wills state that no bond shall be required. The reason for omitting a bond is two-fold. The Will maker chooses someone he Trusts to administer the estate, so he does not think a bond is necessary. And there are economic reasons. The cost of the bond is paid for by the estate, and ultimately the amount inherited is reduced by the amount paid for the bond.

The Court will require a bond of any estate that is greater than $10,000 (after payment of expenses and the Family Allowance) unless the Will excuses the Personal Representative from giving bond, or unless all interested people sign a waiver releasing him from bond. Even if no bond is required, you have the right to petition (ask) the Court to order a bond whenever you are concerned about the safety of estate property (Est. & Trusts 5-604, 6-102).

✧ RIGHT TO COPY OF INVENTORY

The Personal Representative who is conducting a Regular Probate Administration must prepare an inventory of all of the assets of the Probate estate within 3 months of his appointment. The inventory must list all real and personal property owned by the decedent. That includes monies that was owed to the decedent, furs and jewelry, but not his wearing apparel, nor items used by the decedent's family such as food supplies. Monies owed on any item such as a mortgage, or a car loan, must also be listed. The Register will appoint an official appraiser to determine the value of items such as motor vehicles, jewelry, or real property. The Personal Representative can employ a special appraiser instead of using the official appraiser. If you are not satisfied with the value assigned to any item, you can ask to have the item re-appraised (Est. & Trusts 7-201, 7-202, 7-204).

The Personal Representative who is conducting a Modified Administration will file a Final Report within 10 months of being appointed. The Final Report is a combination inventory and accounting. The Personal Representative is not required to give you a formal inventory (or accounting) prior to that time, unless you ask for one.

The purpose of conducting a Modified Administration is to reduce the time (and expense) of administering the estate. A Modified Administration cannot be conducted unless you agree to it. If you think you may want a formal inventory and accounting, then it is best not to agree to a Modified Administration (Est. & Trust 5-702, 5-706).

No inventory need be filed for a Small Estate Administration. The Petition For Administration will give the value of the estate. You can get a copy of the Petition and if you are concerned about the way the property is evaluated, you can ask the Register of Wills to have the property appraised.

✧ RIGHT TO KNOW THE ATTORNEY'S FEES

The job of administering the decedent's estate is complex and there could be liability associated with the job of Personal Representative. For example, if an Inheritance Tax is due and the Personal Representative distributes property before seeing to it that the tax is paid, then he can be made to pay that tax penalty himself (Tax-Gen. 7-216). The Personal Representative has the right to employ an attorney to guide him through the Probate procedure to make sure that the Probate is conducted properly and with no personal liability to the Personal Representative. His attorney's fee are a proper charge to the Probate estate (Est. & Trusts 7-602).

You, as a beneficiary, have the right to know how much the estate will be charged for his services. Ask the Personal Representative to give you a copy of the retainer agreement, so that you will know how much is being charged. If you think the fee too high, you can call different law firms and ask what they charge to Probate an estate with similar assets, and that will give you some idea of the going rate. If after doing some "comparison shopping" you still believe the fee is unreasonable, you can negotiate to lower the fee. The Court must approve attorney fees so, if you are unsuccessful with the negotiation, you can express your concerns to the Court.

✧ RIGHT TO APPROVE FEES

The Personal Representative who is conducting a Regular or Modified Administration is entitled to a ***commission*** (fee or compensation) for administering the estate. If he is also a beneficiary of the estate he may decide not to take a commission and just take his inheritance. The reason may be economic. Any fee the Representative takes is taxable as ordinary income, but monies inherited are not taxable to him as a beneficiary. Ask the Personal Representative to tell you, in writing, whether he intends to charge a commission, and if so, how much.

There are statutory guidelines for what is a "reasonable" commission. For estates of $20,000 or less the commission may not be more than 9% of the value of the estate. For estate that are greater than $20,000, the commission is $1,800 plus 3.6% of any amount over that value (Est. & Trusts 7-601).

There are no statutory guidelines for what is reasonable for attorney's fees. Unless the fee is stated in the Will, the Court will determine what is reasonable. The only exception is when the combined payment to the Personal Representative <u>and</u> to his attorney are not greater than the amount stated in the above paragraph, and all unpaid creditors and all the beneficiaries of the estate agree, in writing, to the payment (Est. & Trusts 7-604).

No Commissions are allowed for the Personal Representative of a Small Estate Administration; however his attorney is entitled to a reasonable fee.

✧ RIGHT TO AN ACCOUNTING

THE REGULAR ADMINISTRATION

Before closing the estate of a Regular Administration the Personal Representative must give the beneficiaries a full accounting. The accounting should start with the inventory value of the estate and end with the amount presently on hand. If the estate has significant assets, you may want your own accountant to look over the accounting.

The Personal Representative can file an accounting and close out the estate any time after he is sure that all claims have been filed against the estate. This is usually 6 months from the date of death. If a federal Estate Tax Return must be filed, then it will probably take more than a year before the Personal Representative receives tax clearance from the IRS and can close out the estate. The beneficiaries are entitled to their first accounting within 9 months of the appointment of the Personal Representative. The Personal Representative must file an accounting every 6 months thereafter until the estate is closed (Est. & Trusts 7-305).

THE MODIFIED ADMINISTRATION

As mentioned, no formal accounting is necessary for a Modified Administration, however, the Personal Representative must file a Final Report within 10 months from his date of appointment and he must distribute the property no later than 12 months after his appointment. The Final Report is essentially an accounting of monies spent and the proposed distribution of whatever assets remain. You, as a beneficiary, are entitled to see a copy of the Final Report, and to raise an objection if you do not agree with the Report as presented (Est. & Trusts 5-704, 5-707).

THE SMALL ESTATE ACCOUNTING

No formal accounting is required of the Personal Representative who is conducting a Small Estate Administration, however, he must file a Certificate of Compliance no later than 60 days after the deadline for filing a claim against the estate. The Certificate of Compliance will state that all bills have been paid and whatever is left, has either been distributed, or will be distributed to the beneficiaries within 30 days of filing the Certificate of Compliance. That means that you as a beneficiary should have your share of the estate no later than 8 months after the date of death. You can ask the Personal Representative for a copy of the Certificate, and of course you can raise an objection if you do not think you have received your fair share of the estate.

✧ RIGHT TO AGREE TO DISTRIBUTION

The Personal Representative should tell you how he intends to distribute the estate once all bills are paid. Specific gifts made in the Will are of course distributed as per the terms of the Will, but some items, such as personal property, might need to be divided in approximately equal shares to several beneficiaries. For a Regular Administration you will have written notice of the proposed distribution and 30 days to file an objection if you disagree with the proposed distribution.

The Personal Representative will try to get all of the beneficiaries to agree to the proposed distribution, but if he is unsuccessful, he will ask the Court to set a hearing on the matter. It is important for you to be present at the hearing so that you can explain how you wish to have the property divided. The Court will decide the matter using whatever method he thinks appropriate, from appointing two people who have no interest in the matter to divide the property, to having the property sold and dividing the money equally (Est. & Trusts 9-104, 9-112)

✧ RIGHT TO RECEIVE A DEBT FREE INHERITANCE

About the last thing a beneficiary wants to hear when he finally receives his inheritance, is that there is some unfinished business, or worse yet that monies need to be paid from the inheritance he received. But that is just what could happen if the Personal Representative distributes the money before everyone is paid.

You can protect yourself from this unhappy situation by checking to see that the Personal Representative gave proper notice to all of the decedent's creditors, and then verifying that they were paid. You should ask to see a copy of all of the tax returns that were filed, and verify that any monies that were due have been paid.

It may be prudent to ask the Personal Representative to keep the estate open until the Statute of Limitation for filing a creditor claim has passed, namely, until 6 months from the date of death has passed (Est. & Trusts 10-102).

IT'S YOUR RIGHT - DON'T BE INTIMIDATED

As a beneficiary, you have many legal rights, but you may feel uncomfortable asserting those rights with a friend or family member who is Personal Representative. Don't be. It's your money and your legal right to be kept informed. Be especially firm if the Personal Representative waves you off with:

"You've known me for years. Surely you trust me."

People who are trustworthy, don't ask to be trusted. They do what is right. The very fact that the Personal Representative is resisting, is a red flag. In such situation, you can explain that it is not a matter of trust, but a matter of what is your legal right.

At the same time, keep things in perspective. Your relationship with the Personal Representative may be more important to you than the money you inherit. The job of settling an estate can be complex and demanding. If the Personal Representative is getting the job done, then let him know that you appreciate his efforts.

THE CHECK LIST

We have discussed many things that need to be done when someone dies in the state of Maryland. The next page contains a check list that you may find helpful.

You can check those items that you need to do, and then cross them off the list once they are done. We made the list as comprehensive as possible, so many items may not apply in your case. In such case, you can cross them off the list or mark them ***N/A*** (not applicable).

Things to do

FUNERAL ARRANGEMENTS TO BE MADE

- ☐ AUTOPSY ☐ ANATOMICAL GIFT
- ☐ DISPOSITION OF BODY OR ASHES

DEATH CERTIFICATE

GIVE COPY TO: ______________________________

____

NOTICE OF DEATH

PEOPLE TO BE NOTIFIED ______________________________

COMPANIES TO NOTIFY

- → ☐ TELEPHONE COMPANY
  - → ☐ LOCAL CARRIER → ☐ LONG DISTANCE ☐ CELLULAR
- → ☐ NEWSPAPER (OBITUARY PRINTED) FUNERAL HOME
- ☐ NEWSPAPER CANCELLED ☐ deposit refund
- → ☐ SOCIAL SECURITY
- ☐ INTERNET SERVER
- ☐ TELEVISION CABLE COMPANY
- ☐ POWER & LIGHT ☐ deposit refund
- ☐ POST OFFICE
- ☐ OTHER UTILITIES (GAS, WATER) ☐ deposit refund
- → ☐ PENSION PLAN CSRS (US GOVT)
- → ☐ ANNUITY LINCOLN NATIONAL
- → ☐ HEALTH INSURANCE COMPANY Blue Cross
- ☐ LIFE INSURANCE COMPANY
- ☐ HOME INSURANCE COMPANY STATE FARM
- → ☐ MOTOR VEHICLE INSURANCE COMPANY
- ☐ CONDOMINIUM OR HOMEOWNER ASSOCIATION
- ☐ CANCEL SERVICE CONTRACT ☐ deposit refund
- → ☐ CREDIT CARD COMPANIES ______________________________

____

____

Things to do

REMOVE DECEDENT AS BENEFICIARY OF:

- ☐ WILL ☐ INSURANCE POLICY ☐ PENSION PLAN
- ☐ BANK OR IRA ACCOUNT ☐ SECURITY

DEBTS

PAY DECEDENT'S DEBTS (AMOUNT & CREDITOR)

CREDIT CARD BILLS

COLLECT MONIES OWED TO DECEDENT (AMOUNT & DEBTOR)

TAXES

- ☐ FILE FINAL FEDERAL INCOME TAX RETURN
- ☐ FILE FINAL STATE INCOME TAX RETURN
- ☐ RECEIVE INCOME TAX REFUND
- ☐ FILE ESTATE TAX RETURN

PROPERTY TO BE TRANSFERRED

- ☐ PERSONAL EFFECTS
- ☐ MOTOR VEHICLE
- ☐ BANK ACCOUNT
- ☐ CREDIT UNION ACCOUNT
- ☐ IRA ACCOUNT
- ☐ SECURITIES
- ☐ BROKERAGE ACCOUNT
- ☐ INSURANCE PROCEEDS
- ☐ HOMESTEAD
- ☐ TIME SHARE
- ☐ OTHER REAL PROPERTY
- ☐ CONTENTS OF SAFE DEPOSIT BOX

OTHER THINGS TO DO

WHAT TO KEEP — WHAT TO THROW AWAY

Once the Probate procedure is over, you will be left with many documents and wonder which you need to keep:

COURT DOCUMENTS

You should keep a copy of the inventory to establish the value of property that you inherit. That value becomes your basis for any Capital Gains tax that you may need to pay in the future. Other than the inventory, there is no reason to keep any Court document, provided you are satisfied with the way things were done; and do not intend to take action against the Personal Representative, or his attorney. The Register of Wills keeps the Probate file on record, so if for some reason you later need a copy of a Probate document, you can get it from the Register.

PERSONAL DOCUMENTS

You may wish to keep the decedent's personal papers (birth certificate, marriage certificate, naturalization papers, army records, religious documents, etc.) for your own personal records. You may want to keep the decedent's medical records in the event that member of the family needs to check out a genetic disease.

TAX RECORDS

The IRS has up to three years to collect additional taxes, and you have up to 7 years to claim a loss from a worthless security, so you should keep the decedent's tax file for seven years from the date of filing the return. You can learn more about which records to keep from the IRS publication 552. You can get the publication by calling the IRS at (800) 829-3676 or you can download it from their Web site:

IRS WEB SITE
http://www.irs.gov

Preneed Arrangements 7

Death is a wake-up call because once someone close to us dies we are reminded of our own mortality. Many of us believe that death can be put off, but the inevitable is inevitable. Although we cannot change the fact of our death, we have the power to control the circumstances of our death by making preneed arrangements.

Preneed arrangements can be made so that you are buried in the manner you wish and where you wish. You can make arrangements that direct the kind of medical treatments you want to be given in the event you become seriously ill.

You can legally appoint someone to make your medical decisions in the event you are too ill to speak for yourself. If you let that person know how you feel about life support systems, autopsies and anatomical gifts then that person will be authorized to act on your behalf and will see to it that your wishes are carried out.

As this chapter will show, it is relatively simple and inexpensive to make such preneed arrangements.

MAKING BURIAL ARRANGEMENTS

When making burial arrangements for the decedent, you may decide to purchase one or more burial spaces nearby for yourself or other family members. If the decedent was buried in the family plot, then this is the time to take inventory of the number of spaces left and who in the family expects to use those spaces.

If all of the spaces are taken and if you plan to be cremated, then as explained in Chapter 1, some cemeteries will allow an urn to be placed in an occupied family plot. You can call the cemetery and ask them to explain their policy as it relates to the burial of an urn in a currently occupied grave site or mausoleum. If this is not an option, and the cemetery of your choice has a columbarium, you might consider purchasing a space at this time. If you wish to have your cremains scattered, then you need to let your next of kin know where and how this is to be done.

It is important to let your family know of your wishes for your final disposition. If you do not, then the person with authority to decide the matter for you is determined by Maryland statute (Bus. Reg. 5-509). Priority for making your final disposition is as follows:

1st your spouse 2nd your adult child
3rd your parent 4th your adult brother or sister
5th anyone acting as your representative under written authorization given by you
6th A guardian who was appointed by the court prior to the death
7th Anyone who assumes the responsibility provided they state in writing that they made a good faith effort to contact everyone else with priority.

Special Situation

VETERAN OR VETERAN'S SPOUSE

If you are an honorably discharged veteran, you have the right to be buried in a Veterans National Cemetery. You cannot reserve a grave site in advance. If your Veteran spouse was buried in a Veterans National Cemetery, then you have the right to be buried in that same grave site unless soil conditions require a separate grave site.

If you wish to be buried in a Veterans National Cemetery, then check on current availability (see page 15 for telephone numbers). Let your next of kin know your choice of cemetery.

To establish your eligibility your next of kin will need to provide the following information:

- the veteran's rank, serial, Social Security and VA claim numbers
- the branch of service; the date and place of entry into and separation from the service

The next of kin will also need to provide the VA with a copy of the veteran's official military discharge document bearing an official seal or a DD 214 form.

If you wish to be buried in a national cemetery, then make all of these items readily accessible to your family.

If you are financially able, in addition to purchasing a burial space, consider purchasing a Preneed Funeral Plan. It will be easier on your family emotionally and financially if you make your own funeral arrangements. If you do not have sufficient cash on hand for the kind of funeral you desire, then many funeral directors offer an installment payment plan.

Once you decide on a plan, the funeral director will present you with a contract. The print may be small, but it is worth your effort to read it before signing. If the contract is written in "legalese" then either consult with your attorney before signing it or ask as many questions of the funeral director as is necessary to make the terms of the contract clear to you. If you are not satisfied with the way a certain section of the contract is written then add an addendum to the contract that explains, in plain English, your understanding of that passage. If you are concerned about something that is not mentioned in the contract, then insist that the contract be amended to include that item. In particular, check to see whether the contract answers the following questions.

Does the contract cover all costs?

The contract should contain an itemized list stating exactly what goods and services are included in the sales price. Ask the funeral director whether there will be any additional cost when you die. For example, if you have not purchased a burial space, then that cost needs to be factored in. If you made provision for a burial space, then you need to let the funeral director know where you have arranged to be buried. If you have not made such provision, then the funeral director can assist you in making burial arrangements.

Is the price guaranteed?

Some Preneed plans have a fixed price for the goods and services you chose. You are guaranteed that the goods and services will be provided upon your death, regardless of when you finally die. If the price for the goods and services that you have chosen under the Preneed contract is not fixed, then the company can charge additional monies upon your death. In these days of an ever increasing life expectancy, it is important that such a contract clearly state how the price will be determined when the contract is finally put into effect.

How are your contract funds protected?

Maryland law requires funeral homes to protect funds paid by the consumer of a Preneed Funeral Plan by placing the 80% of the money prepaid by the buyer for the casket and 100% of monies paid for the rest of the goods and services in an interest bearing, escrow or trust account. The seller is required to file an annual report, certified by a Certified Public Accountant, showing that the funeral home has complied with the law (Health-Occup. 7-405).

The law requires that the deposit be made within 10 days of signing the contract. Before signing have the funeral home give you the name of the bank. Have the contract state that they will furnish you with proof of deposit within 10 days.

Maryland statute requires that all monies in the escrow or trust account together with any earned interest, be returned to the buyer if the seller goes out of business. The only problem is that the most costly item is usually the casket and the seller is required to deposit only 80% of monies paid. If the funeral home goes out of business, you will probably lose 20% of the price of the casket. Which leads to the next and most important question, namely whether you are doing business with a reputable firm.

Is the funeral firm reputable?

In Maryland, anyone who offers Preneed contracts to the public must be licensed to do so (Health Occup. 7-504). It is prudent to take the time to call the investigation division of the Maryland State Board of Morticians at (410) 764-4792. Ask whether the funeral home is properly licensed, how long they have been in business, and whether any complaints have been filed against them.

Can you cancel the contract?

Maryland law gives the buyer (or his legal representative) the right to cancel the entire contract and receive all monies paid, plus any accumulated interest (Health-Occup. 7-405).

THE IRREVOCABLE CONTRACT

People who are applying for, or receiving, Medicaid, Supplemental Security Income ("SSI") or other public assistance program have limits on the amount of assets that they may own. If someone purchases a Preneed Funeral Plan, then the monies paid into the plan count as an asset because the purchaser of the plan can revoke the contract and get his money back. Understanding the problem, Maryland law allows a person who is applying for or receiving Medicaid or SSI or any benefit plan that restricts eligibility to those with limited assets, to purchase an ***irrevocable*** plan (one that can't be cancelled). The monies paid must be placed into an irrevocable trust until such time as they are needed to fulfill the contract.

Even if you are in good health at this time, it is a good idea to have your contract provide that you can make your agreement irrevocable, if at any time you need to apply for a public assistance program.

Suppose you die in another state or country?

It is a good idea to have the contract spell out what provision will be made in the event that you move to another state or in the event you happen to die in another state or country. Many funeral firms are part of a national funeral service corporation with funeral firms located throughout the United States. You may be able to have the contract provide that there will be no additional charge if the contract is performed by one of the funeral firms owned by the parent company.

Can the plan be changed after your death?

It may happen that your heirs need to cancel the plan after your death because:

- your body is missing or cannot be recovered, or
- you were buried by another funeral home because your family was unaware of your Preneed contract at the time of your death, or
- you died in another country and were buried there.

Or perhaps your heirs decide on a plan different than the one you purchased. Funeral firms generally allow heirs to make changes to the plan you paid for such as:

- purchasing a more expensive plan and paying the difference
- changing to a lesser plan and receiving a refund.

Under Maryland law, your Personal Representative has the same right as you do to cancel the contract and receive the monies you paid (Health-Occup. 7-405). You may wonder why anyone would think of changing the decedent's funeral plan, but consider that in today's market, it is not uncommon for a Preneed contract to cost several thousand dollars. A top end funeral complete with solid bronze casket can cost upwards of $40,000.

And there may be other motivations. Consider the case of Mona, a difficult woman with a personality that can only be described as "sour." Her husband deserted her after four years of marriage leaving her to raise their son, Lester, by herself. Once Lester was grown, Mona made it clear to him that she had done her job and now he was on his own. Lester could have used some help. He married and had three children. One of his children suffered with asthma and it was a constant struggle to keep up with the medical bills.

Mona believed in being good to herself. She did not intend to, nor did she, leave much money when she died. She knew that Lester would not be able to afford a "proper" burial for her, so she purchased a funeral plan and paid close to $18,000 for it. She was pleased when the funeral director told her that the monies would be kept safely in an escrow account until the time they were needed.

Lester was not familiar with Maryland law, so when Mona died he asked an attorney at the Legal Aid office to determine whether the Preneed contract was revocable.

It was.

You know the ending to this story.

If you are concerned that you get the exact type of funeral that you want, with no changes, then there are several ways to do so. You could purchase a life insurance policy payable to your estate with specific instructions in your Will about how your funeral is to be conducted. It may take some time to probate your estate, so you may want to provide a copy of the funeral instructions to your Personal Representative and to the funeral home.

There are other ways to accomplish this goal. It is best to consult with your attorney to set up a plan best suited for your needs.

You may be thinking "Revocable, Irrevocable. All this contract stuff is giving me a headache. Why can't I just set aside some money and let my kids figure it out?"

The problem with that approach is that life may be unkind and you leave this place with little or no funds to bury you. To avoid the problem, you could purchase a life insurance policy to fund your funeral and burial, naming one or two trusted family members as the beneficiary of the policy. It is important that the person who is to receive the insurance funds clearly understands why he/she is named as beneficiary of the policy. It is equally important that the beneficiary agree to use the monies for the intended purpose.

It isn't so much that a family member is not trustworthy as it is that they may not understand what you intended — especially in those cases where other funds are available to pay for the funeral. Too often insurance funds are left to a sibling who then refuses to contribute to the cost of the funeral saying in effect "Dad wanted me to have this money — that's why he left it to me."

To avoid a misunderstanding, put it in writing. It need not be a formal contract. It could be something as simple as a letter to the insurance beneficiary, with copies to your next of kin. The next page contains a sample letter.

Dear Romita,

I purchased a $20,000 insurance policy today naming you as beneficiary of the policy. As we discussed this money is to be used to pay for the following:

- *my funeral and grave site*
- *my headstone*
- *perpetual care for my grave*
- *airfare for each of my grandchildren to attend the funeral*
- *dinner for the family after the wake*
- *lunch for the family after the funeral*

If there is any money left over, please accept it as my thanks for all the effort spent on my behalf.

Love,
Dad

P.S. I am sending a copy of this letter to your brother so that he will know that all arrangements have been made.

Whether or not you arrange to pay for your burial or funeral, you need to let your next of kin know your feelings about the burial procedure. Let your family know whether you wish to be cremated or buried. If you wish to have a religious service, then let your family know the type of service and where it is to be held. Let the family know where you wish to be buried, or if you intend to be cremated, then where to place the ashes.

ANATOMICAL GIFTS

If you wish to make an anatomical gift, you can make that donation by completing a donor card or by letting your family know that you wish to make a donation of some or all of your body parts. You can use the ANATOMICAL GIFT BY A LIVING DONOR form as printed in the Maryland statutes (Est. & Trusts 4-505) or you can obtain a donor form from the motor vehicle bureau.

If you signed a donor card that is valid in another state, then that donation will be recognized in Maryland (Health-General 4-505 (f)). You can even include an anatomical gift as part of your Will (Est. & Trusts 4-505 (a)), but the problem with putting the gift in your Will is that you may long since been buried before anyone looks at your Will. The better route is to sign the Maryland statutory form and let your family know that it is your desire to make such a gift.

If you are aged, and in poor health, the local Organ Procurement Organization will probably not consider your body for transplantation of body parts, but you can still donate your body for education and research.

If you do not wish to make an anatomical gift, then let your family know how you feel.

AUTOPSIES

As discussed in Chapter 1, some autopsies are optional. If you have strong feelings about allowing an optional autopsy or not allowing the procedure, then let your family know how you feel.

Of course, there are problems with just telling someone how you feel about your burial arrangements, autopsies, and anatomical gifts:

THE PERSON DOES NOT CARRY OUT YOUR WISHES

Without written instructions, your next of kin will decide and then authorize the disposition of your remains. Whether they authorize an anatomical gift or an autopsy may depend more about how they feel about the procedure than what you wish.

Sometimes the person you tell may not understand what you said or perhaps they hear only what they want to hear. An example that comes to mind is the mother who complained that she felt like a burden to her children. She would often say "When I die, burn my body and throw my ashes out to sea." Her children paid no attention. No one asked, nor did they even think about, what she may have really wanted. When she died she was given a full funeral and buried in a local cemetery.

Even if you tell someone and trust that person to carry out your wishes, it could be that the person you confide in cannot carry out your instructions. For example, if you tell your spouse what arrangements to make, then he/she may become incapacitated or die before you do; or perhaps you both die simultaneously in a natural disaster or in a plane crash.

YOU TELL THE WRONG PERSON

You may tell someone who does not have authority to carry out your wishes. That was the case with James. Once his wife died, he moved to a retirement community where he lived for 15 years until his death.

James had two sons who lived in different states. Although he loved his sons, he had difficulty talking to either of them about serious matters. It was easier for him to talk with his friends in the retirement community. They often spoke about dying and how they felt about different burial arrangements. James would reminisce about his youth and growing up in a farming community in the plains state of Kansas. "I was happy and free. Out there you had room to breathe. It would be nice to be buried there — peaceful and spacious."

When he died, his friends told his sons about their father's desire to be buried in Kansas. They met the suggestion with scepticism and pragmatism:

"Dad didn't say anything like that to me."

"It would cost us double, if we had to arrange for burial in another state. I'm sure he didn't have that kind of expense in mind."

WHO WANTS TO TALK ABOUT IT?

For many people the main problem with telling someone what to do when you die is talking about your death. It may be an uncomfortable, if not unpleasant, subject for you to bring up, and for your family to discuss. If this is the case, then consider putting the information in writing and give the instructions to the person who will have the job of carrying out your wishes.

APPOINTING A HEALTH CARE AGENT

You can legally appoint someone to carry out your wishes relating to the care of your person, by signing a document called an ***Advance Directive***. Maryland statute (Health-Gen. 5-603) contains a statutory form that you can use to appoint a ***Health Care Agent*** to make your medical decisions in the event that you are too ill to do so yourself.

The statutory form contains a ***Living Will*** that tells your Health Care Agent whether you do (or do not) want life support systems to be used in the event that you are dying and there is no hope for your recovery. If you want to make an anatomical gift, then you can give your Health Care Agent authority to consent to the gift on your behalf (see page 4). If you do not wish to make an anatomical gift, then you can direct your Health Care Agent to not allow the procedure.

You can prepare your own Advance Directive by copying the statutory form of the Advance Directive. You can look up the statute by going to the nearest courthouse law library. You can also download the form from the Internet. See page x of the Introduction to this book for information about how to look up a statute on the Internet.

You can have your attorney prepare an Advance Directive especially designed to meet your special needs. For example, you can include funeral or burial arrangements as part of your Advance Directive. It makes more sense to put these instructions in your Medical Directive rather than in your Will. Your Will may not be found for several days after your death, but your Advance Directive is available to your Health Care Agent as soon as it is signed.

If you do not appoint someone to be your Health Care Agent and give that person authority to act in accordance with your Advance Directive, then the person with authority to direct your medical treatment is determined by Maryland Statute (Health-Gen. 5-605). The statute establishes the following order of priority:

- 1st the court appointed guardian (if any)
- 2nd the patient's spouse
- 3rd the patient's adult child
- 4th a parent of the patient
- 5th an adult brother or sister
- 6th a relative who has had regular contact with the patient
- 7th a close friend

If ever you are too ill to make your own medical decisions, your doctor will contact the person with highest priority. If that person is not reasonably available, or if he is unwilling or not competent to make medical decisions for you, then the doctor will contact the next person with priority. If there are several people with equal authority and they disagree about the proposed treatment, then the doctor may decide to ask the Court to appoint someone to be your Guardian and make your medical decisions.

If the above order of priority is not as you wish, or if there is someone you wish to exclude altogether from making your health care decisions, then it is important to sign an Advance Directive and appoint the person of your choice to act as your Health Care Agent. If not, life decisions made for you, may not be as you would have wished.

George is a case in point. His wife suffered from Alzheimer's disease. He cared for her at home for as long as he was able, but finally, it was too much for him and he placed her in a local nursing facility. He and his two daughters visited her frequently, even though she scarcely recognized them.

Emily's husband also suffered from Alzheimer's disease and was at the same facility. George and Emily met at the nursing home support group and found that they had much in common. After visiting with their respective spouses they would go to the local coffee shop. One thing led to another, and soon they were an item.

George's daughters were not happy with the coupling. They criticized everything about Emily, from the way she dressed to her table manners. When Emily moved in with George, his daughters made cutting remarks about Emily's moral character. Emily didn't take it personally. She believed the girls were more concerned about their inheritance than George's happiness. A second marriage might cut into what they already considered to be rightfully theirs.

Not that George and Emily planned to wed. They both loved their respective spouses and had no intention of trying to obtain a divorce. Their understanding was that if and when they both were single, they would discuss marriage at that time.

Meanwhile, George and Emily enjoyed each other, feeling and acting like a couple of teenagers. But their happiness lasted only a few months. George suffered a stroke while driving a car. His injuries from the accident combined with the severity of the stroke made for a bleak prognosis. The doctors said George would die unless they put him on a ventilator and inserted a feeding tube. Even with life support systems, it was not expected that he would ever come out of the coma.

Emily pleaded to keep him alive. "Let's try everything. If he doesn't improve we can always discontinue the life support systems later."

George's daughters did not see it that way. "Why torture him with needles and tubes? Let him pass on peacefully."

George never signed a Living Will so no one knew whether he would or would nor want artificial life support systems. He never appointed anyone to be his Health Care Agent to make his health care decisions in the event he was unable to do so. In the absence of an Advance Directive, the doctors had no choice. Under Maryland law, the daughters were 3rd in priority. Emily was not a member of the family, so she had no priority at all.

George died.

Everyman's Estate Plan 8

The first six chapters of this book describe how to wind up the affairs of the decedent. As you read those chapters, you learned about the kinds of problems that can occur when settling the decedent's estate. It is relatively simple for you to set up an Estate Plan so that your family members are not burdened with similar problems. An ***Estate Plan*** is the arranging of your finances for maximum control and protection during your lifetime, and at the same time ensuring that your property will be transferred quickly and at little cost to your heirs.

If you think that only wealthy people need to prepare an Estate Plan, you are mistaken. Each year, heirs of relatively modest estates, spend thousands of dollars to settle an Estate. A bit of planning could have eliminated most, if not all, of the expense and hassle suffered by those families.

The suggestions in this chapter are designed to assist the average person in preparing a practical and inexpensive Estate Plan, so we named this chapter EVERYMAN'S ESTATE PLAN.

Once you create your own Estate Plan, you can be assured that your family will not be left with more problems than happy memories of you.

AVOIDING PROBATE

TRUE OR FALSE?

( ) If you have a Will, then there will need to be a Probate administration.

( ) Probate is only necessary if you don't have a Will.

( ) Probate is necessary if you leave anything worth more than $30,000.

If you answered false to all of the above, you are either a lawyer, or you carefully read the chapters 5 and 6.

For those who do not enjoy "Pop Quizzes," please forgive our reversion to educator (or maybe pedant). The point we were attempting to make is that:

> Whether a Probate procedure is necessary has nothing to do with whether there is a Will, or even how much money is involved. The determining factor is how the property is titled (owned).

There are three ways to title property:

- jointly with another
- in trust for another
- in your name only.

In general, property held jointly or in trust for someone goes directly to the intended beneficiary without the need for Probate. There may need to be a Probate procedure if property is held in the decedent's name only.

In this chapter we explore the pros and cons of titling property in each of the three ways, beginning with holding property jointly with another.

OWNERSHIP OF BANK ACCOUNTS

You can arrange to have all of your bank accounts set up so that should you die, the money goes directly to a beneficiary. For example, suppose all you own is a bank account and you want whatever you have in this account to go to your son and daughter when you die. You might think that a simple solution is to put each child's name on the account as joint tenants with right of survivorship, but first consider the problems associated with a joint account:

☒ POTENTIAL LIABILITY

If you hold a bank account jointly with your adult child and that child is sued or gets a divorce, the child may need to disclose his ownership of the joint account. In such a case, you may find yourself spending money to prove that the account was established for your convenience only and that all of the money in that account really belongs to you.

☒ OVERREACHING

If you set up a joint account with your child so that the child has authority to withdraw funds from the account, then funds could be withdrawn without your knowledge or authorization. If you open a joint account with two of your children, then there is the problem of what happens to the funds after your death. Should you die, then under Maryland law that account belongs to the surviving joint owners (Finan. Inst. 1-204). Each joint owner has access to the joint account. After your death the first child to the bank may decide to withdraw all of the money and that will, at the very least, cause hard feelings between them.

Holding a bank account jointly with your beneficiary eliminates the need for Probate, but at the cost of control of the funds during your lifetime. There are two ways to title your bank account so that it passes directly to your beneficiary, but without access to that property during your lifetime:

THE IN TRUST FOR ("ITF") ACCOUNT: You can direct a financial institution to hold your account ***In Trust For*** ("ITF") one or more beneficiaries that you name.

THE PAY ON DEATH ("POD") ACCOUNT: You can have a contract with the bank that directs the bank to ***Pay On Death*** ("POD") all of the money in the account to one or more beneficiaries that you name.

With both the ITF and POD account:

- ⇨ During his lifetime the owner of the account is free to change beneficiaries without asking the beneficiary's permission to do so.
- ⇨ The beneficiary does not have any right to the account until the owner of the account dies.
- ⇨ If there are two or more beneficiaries, then once the owner dies, the funds are divided equally among the beneficiaries of the account.
- ⇨ If there are two or more beneficiaries of the account, and one of them dies, the remaining beneficiaries will inherit the account, unless the owner of the account makes some other provision with the bank
- ⇨ If no beneficiary survives the owner of the account, then the account will go become part of the owner's Probate Estate. If the account is held jointly with rights of survivorship, and no beneficiary of the account survives, the funds will go to the Estate of the last owner of the account to die (Finan. Inst. 1-204).

The Maryland law for securities is much the same as the statutes for bank accounts. You can arrange to have a security (a stock, bond or brokerage account) transferred to a beneficiary upon your death. You can instruct the holder of the security to PAY ON DEATH ("POD") or TRANSFER ON DEATH ("TOD") to a named beneficiary. For example, a security can be titled as:

TIM REILLY and OLIVIA REILLY, JOINT TENANTS
TRANSFER ON DEATH TO STUART REILLY

Stuart has no right to the security until both his parents die. The parents are free to change the beneficiary of the security at any time during their lifetime. If no change is made, Stuart will inherit the security once both parents are deceased. All he need do to transfer the securities to his name is produce a certified copy of the death certificate. If Stuart dies before his parents and no other provision made, then the security will go to the Estate of the last parent to die (Est. & Trusts 16-105, 16-106, 16-107).

If your Estate consists only of bank accounts and/or securities, and you want all of your property to go to one or two beneficiaries without the need for Probate, but with maximum control and protection of your funds during your lifetime, then holding your property in any of these beneficiary forms:

"In Trust For"
"Pay-On-Death"
"Transfer-On-Death"

should accomplish your goal.

THE GIFT TO THE MINOR CHILD

At the beginning of this chapter, we identified two problems with a joint account: potential liability if the joint owner is sued and overreaching by the joint owner. If you wish to make a gift to a minor child, then that presents still another problem. The ITF, POD and TOD account avoid the problem of potential liability and overreaching, but if the beneficiary of such account is a minor, there is the problem of the child having access to a large sum of money. A company in possession of the funds may give amounts up to $5,000 to whoever has custody of the child. The company is not required to do so and may decide to ask Court permission before they transfer funds. It is mandatory for the company to seek Court permission for amounts over $5,000 (Est. & Trusts 13-501). The Court will probably require that a Guardian be appointed to protect the funds until the child reaches 18.

This presents a dilemma. If the amount given is no greater than $5,000, and the company decides to give the money to the parent, all of the funds may be spent to care for the child. The child may never even know of your gift. You may think it best that the child inherits more than $5,000; this way a Court will see to it that the monies are held safely till the child reaches 18. But that only presents a new set of problems. It takes time, effort and money to set up a guardianship. If you leave the child a significant amount of money, then the Guardian has the right to be paid to manage those funds. It could happen that the cost of the guardianship significantly reduces the amount of money inherited by the child. There are ways to avoid the problem of having a Guardian appointed to care for property inherited by a child, and yet ensuring that the monies are protected. We will discuss those methods, in detail, in the next chapter.

THE GIFT OF REAL PROPERTY

As explained in Chapter 5, if you own real property together with another, then who owns the property upon your death depends on how the Grantee is identified on the face of the deed. If you compare the Grantee clause of the deed to the examples on pages 99 through 105 you can determine who will inherit the property should you die. If you are not satisfied with the way the property will be inherited, then you need to consult with an attorney to change the deed so that it will conform to your wishes.

If you hold real property in your name only, once you die, a Probate procedure will be necessary in order to transfer the property to the proper beneficiary. If your main objective is to avoid Probate, you can have an attorney change the deed so that it descends to your beneficiary without the need for Probate. As with bank and securities accounts there are different ways to do so, each with its own advantages and disadvantages.

JOINT OWNERSHIP

If you hold property in your name only, and wish to avoid Probate, you can have your deed changed so that you and a beneficiary are joint owners with rights of survivorship. If you do so, should either of you die, the other will own the property 100%. That avoids Probate, but by making that person joint owner, you are, in effect, making a gift of half of the property during your lifetime. You will not be able to sell that property without the beneficiary's permission. And if the beneficiary gives permission and the property is sold, the beneficiary will have the legal right to half of the proceeds of the sale. As explained on the next page, you may be creating tax problems as well.

If you make someone a joint owner who is not a member your immediate family (see Page 135 for a list of exempt family members) and that joint owner dies, you may need to pay an Inheritance Tax on the decedent's "half" of the property unless you can prove to the satisfaction of the Register of Wills, that the decedent's name was put on the deed to avoid Probate and that the property really belongs to you. And, as explained on page 35, you can arrange to sell your home without paying a Capital Gains tax, but if you make someone joint owner of your home who does not live with you, a Capital Gains tax may need to be paid on the joint owner's share of the proceeds should you decide to sell the property.

CAUTION GIFT OF HOMESTEAD

Some elderly parents worry that they may need nursing care at some time in the future and lose all of their life savings to pay for that care. The parent may decide that the best way to avoid Probate and protect the homestead from loss is to transfer the homestead to their child with the understanding that the parent will continue to live there until he/she dies. But this is just trading risks:

RISK OF LOSS

Property transferred to your child could be lost if the child runs into serious financial difficulties or gets sued. This is especially a risk if your child is a professional doctor, nurse, accountant, financial planner, attorney, etc.). If your child is (or gets) married, then this complicates matters even more so. If the child is divorced, the property may need to be included as part of the settlement agreement. This may be to your child's detriment because the child may need to share the value of the property with his/her ex-spouse. If you do not transfer the property, then it cannot become part of the marital equation.

⌧ POSSIBLE LOSS OF GOVERNMENT BENEFITS

If you transfer property, then depending upon the value of the transfer, you could be disqualified from receiving Medicaid or Supplemental Security Income ("SSI") benefits for up to 3 years from the date of transfer to a person; and up to 5 years if you transfer the property to an irrevocable Trust. It could well happen that you might need extended nursing care during that penalty period.

⌧ POSSIBLE GIFT TAX

If the value of the transfer is worth more than $10,000 you need to file a gift tax return. For most of us, this is not a problem because no gift tax need be paid unless the value of the property (plus the value of all gifts in excess of $10,000 per person, per year, that you gave over your lifetime) exceeds the current Gift Tax Exemption (see Page 37). If your estate is in that tax bracket, then you need to be aware that you are "using up" your Exemption Value.

⌧ POSSIBLE CAPITAL GAINS TAX

There is no discussion in Congress to do away with the Capital Gains Tax. If you gift the property to the child, when he sells the property he will be subject to a Capital Gains Tax on the increase in value from the price you paid to the selling price at the time of the sale. If you do not make the gift during your lifetime, the child will inherit the property with a step-up in basis, i.e., he will inherit the property at its market value as of the date of death. Under today's tax structure and continuing until 2009, that step-up in basis is unlimited. If your child sells the property when it is inherited, no Capital Gains Tax is due regardless of how large the step-up in basis. In 2010, there will be a limit on amount that can be inherited free of the Capital Gains Tax but that limit is quite high so for most of us this is not a concern (see Page 38).

⌧ LOSS OF TAX CREDIT

As explained on page 34, certain homestead tax credits are allowed for the aged and disabled who have small incomes. If you are eligible for such tax credit and you transfer your homestead to your child, you will lose this tax break not only for yourself but for your surviving spouse should something happen to you (Tax-Property 7-207, 7-208, 9-104).

Some of the problems associated with an outright gift, such as loss of a tax credit, may be avoided by transferring the property to your child while keeping a Life Estate for yourself (Tax-Property 9-105). But, as with joint ownership, you will not be able to sell or transfer the property during your lifetime unless your child agrees to the transfer. And as with joint ownership, should you sell the property your child is entitled to some part of the proceeds of the sale.

Before making any real property transfer, it is important to consult with your accountant, and/or attorney, and/or certified financial planner, to examine all aspects related to the transfer.

☎ LAWYER OUT OF STATE PROPERTY

Each state is in charge of the way property located in that state is transferred. If you own property in another state (or country) then you need to consult with an attorney in that state (or country) to determine how that property will be transferred to your beneficiaries once you die. Many state laws are similar to Maryland, namely, property held as JOINT TENANTS WITH RIGHT OF SURVIVOR or a LIFE ESTATE INTEREST are transferred without the need for Probate.

If you own property in another state in your name only, or as a TENANT IN COMMON, or if you hold property with your spouse in a community property state, then a Probate procedure may need to be held in that state. If it is necessary to have a Probate procedure in Maryland, then a second Probate procedure may need to be held in the state where the property is located. This could have the effect of doubling the cost of Probate.

Still another problem is the matter of taxes. Inheritance taxes may be due in the state where the property is held. It may be necessary to file a tax return in two states. In addition to increased taxes, this can double the cost of the accounting fees.

You may wish to consult with an attorney for suggestions about how to set up your Estate Plan to avoid such problems.

A full Probate procedure may be necessary if you hold property in your name only or as a Tenant-In-Common. We explored different ways to re-title property to avoid Probate, but these methods may have trade-offs that are unacceptable to you. One way to avoid many of these potential problems is to set up a ***Revocable Living Trust*** (also known as an ***Inter Vivos Trust***).

A Revocable Living Trust is designed to care for your property during your lifetime and then to distribute your property once you die without the need for Probate. You may have been encouraged to set up such a Trust by your financial planner, or attorney, or accountant. Even people of modest means are being encouraged to use a Trust as the basis of their Estate Plan. But Trusts have their pros and cons. Before getting into that, let's first discuss what a Trust is and how it works:

SETTING UP A TRUST

To create a Trust, an attorney prepares the Trust document in accordance with the client's needs and desires. The person who signs the document is called the ***Trustor*** or ***Settlor.*** If the ***Trustor*** also funds the Trust, then he is also referred to as the ***Grantor.*** We will refer to the Revocable Living Trust as the "Living Trust" or just the "Trust" and the person setting up the Trust as the "Grantor." The Trust document identifies who is to be the Trustee (manager) of property placed in the Trust. Usually the Grantor appoints himself as Trustee so that he is in total control of property that he places into the Trust. The Trust document also names a Successor Trustee who will take over the management of the Trust property should the Trustee resign, or become disabled or die.

Once the Trust document is properly signed, the Grantor transfers property into the Trust. The Grantor does this by changing the name on the account from his individual name to his name as Trustee. For example, if Elaine Richards sets up a Trust naming herself as Trustee, and she wishes to place her bank account into the Trust then all she need do is instruct the bank to change the name on the account from ELAINE RICHARDS to:

ELAINE RICHARDS, TRUSTEE of the ELAINE RICHARDS REVOCABLE TRUST AGREEMENT DATED JULY 12, 2001.

When the change is made, all the money in the account becomes Trust property. Elaine (wearing her Trustee hat) has total control of the account, taking money out, and putting money in, as she sees fit. Similarly, if she wants to put real property into the Trust all she need do is have her attorney prepare a new deed with the Grantee identified as ELAINE RICHARDS, TRUSTEE (see page 105 for an example of real property placed into a Trust).

The Trust document states how the Trust property is to be managed during Elaine's lifetime. Should Elaine become disabled the Trust will provide for her Successor Trustee to take over and manage the Trust funds. Because the Trust is revocable, if she wishes, Elaine can terminate the Trust at any time and have all the Trust property returned and placed back into her own individual name. If she does not revoke her Trust during her lifetime, then once she dies the Trust becomes irrevocable, and her Successor Trustee must follow the terms of the Trust Agreement as written. If the Trust says to give the Trust property to certain beneficiaries, then the Successor Trustee will do so; and in most cases without any Probate procedure. If the Trust directs the Successor Trustee to continue to hold property in Trust and use the money to take care of a member of Elaine's family, then the Successor Trustee will do so.

THE GOOD PART

Setting up a Trust has many good features.

☆ TAX SAVINGS:

Many people think that the Estate Tax will be phased out so that by 2010, no Estate Taxes will be due regardless of the size of an estate. That's true for 2010, but the current law covers only the period from 2001 to 2010. The Estate Tax is scheduled to be reinstated on January 1, 2011 and estates worth more than $1,000,000 will once again be subject to a sizeable Estate Tax. A couple with an estate in excess of a million dollars can reduce the risk of an Estate Tax by setting up his and her Trusts, so that each person can take advantage of his own Exemption value (see Page 37).

For example, if a couple own 2 million dollars, they can separate their funds into two Trusts each valued at one million dollars. Each Trust can be set up so that a surviving spouse can use the income from the deceased partner's Trust for living expenses. In this way, their standard of living need not be reduced by separating their funds into two Trusts. Once both partners are deceased, the beneficiaries of their respective Trusts will inherit the funds, hopefully with no Estate Tax due.

If the couple do not set up his/her Trusts and continue to hold their property jointly, then the last to die will own the two million dollars with only one tax Exemption available.

☆ PRIVACY

Your Trust is a private document. No one but your Trustee and your beneficiaries need ever read it. When opening a Trust account, the bank might ask to see your Trust, but you can often restrict their inspection to the first page and signature page of your Trust. If you have a Will, it becomes a public document once you are deceased. Once it is deposited with the Court, anyone can examine the county records, read your Will and see who you did (or did not) provide for. All other Probate documents filed with the Register of Wills (notices, creditor's claims, etc.) are open to public scrutiny. It is not much of a stretch to predict that in the future, Court records will be available on the Internet!

LEASE SAFE DEPOSIT BOX AS TRUSTEE

As explained on page 76, if you hold a safe deposit box in your name only, then once the bank learns of your death, access to the box is restricted. No one can remove anything from the box, other than the Will. A Personal Representative will need to be appointed to take possession of the contents of the safe deposit box. If you have arranged your finances to avoid Probate, then it is self defeating to have entry to a safe deposit box trigger a Probate procedure. One of the benefits of having a Living Trust, is that you can lease the safe deposit box in your name as Trustee. When you lease the safe deposit box you can have an agreement with the bank that they are to allow your Successor Trustee free access to the safe deposit box in the event of your incapacity or death (Finan. Inst. 12-602).

☆ AVOID APPOINTMENT OF A GUARDIAN

Once you have a Trust you do not need to worry about who will take care of your property should you become disabled or too aged to handle your finances. The person you appoint as Successor Trustee will take over the care of the Trust property if you are unable to do so. If you do not have a Trust and you become incapacitated, a Court may need to appoint a Guardian to care for your property. The cost to establish and maintain the Guardianship is charged to you. And that can be even more expensive than a Regular Probate procedure (see Page 231).

☆ CARE FOR FAMILY MEMBER:

You can make provision in your Trust to care for a minor child or family member after you die. If your family member is immature or a born spender, you can set up a Spendthrift Trust to protect him/her from squandering the inheritance. You can direct your Successor Trustee to use Trust funds to pay for the family member's health care, education or living expenses, and nothing more. The Trust can be set up so that the creditors of the family member cannot force the Trustee to use any of the Trust property to pay for monies owed. In this manner you can ensure that the funds will be used for the purpose you intended and nothing more.

☆☆ AVOID PROBATE

In Maryland, Probate can be time consuming and very expensive. Both the Personal Representative and his attorney are entitled to payment for their services. These fees can be significant. It may be necessary to employ accountants and appraisers, as well. If you have property in two states, then two Probate procedures may be necessary (one in each state) and that could have the effect of doubling the cost of Probate. If the Trust is properly drafted and your property placed into the Trust, you should be able to avoid Probate altogether.

THE PROBLEMS

With all these perks, you may be ready to call your attorney to make an appointment to set up a Trust, but before doing so there are a few things you need to consider:

☒ COMPLEXITY

A Trust is a fairly complex document, often 20 pages long. It needs to be that long because you are establishing a vehicle for taking care of your property during your lifetime, as well as after your death. The Trust usually is written in "legalese," so it may take you considerable time and effort to understand it. It is important to have your Trust document prepared by an attorney who has the patience to work with you until you fully understand each paragraph of the document and are satisfied that this is what you want.

☒ TAXES MAY STILL BE A PROBLEM:

While the Grantor is operating the Trust as Trustee, all of the property held in a Revocable Living Trust is taxed as if the Grantor were holding that property in his/her own name. If the value of the Trust property exceeds the Estate and Gift Tax exemption amount (see page 37 for the value), taxes will be due and owing once the Grantor dies. For those in that fortunate tax bracket, an experienced financial planner or tax attorney can suggest other, more advanced, Estate Planning strategies to reduce taxes.

☒ NO CREDITOR PROTECTION

Because property held in a Revocable Living Trust is freely accessible to the Grantor, it is freely accessible to his creditors. And a Trust cannot be set up to protect the Grantor. Maryland courts have ruled that a Grantor can create a Spendthrift Trust for the protection of a beneficiary of the Trust, but not for himself (*Watterson v. Edgerly*, 40 Md. App. 230 (1978), 388 A.2d 934).

⌧ COST

Because of the thoroughness of the document and the fact that it is custom designed for you, a Trust will cost much more to draft than a simple Will. In addition to the initial cost of the Trust, it can be expensive to maintain the Trust should you become disabled or die. Your Successor Trustee has the right to charge for his duties as Trustee, as well as for any specialized service he performs. For example, if you choose an attorney to be Successor Trustee, the attorney has the right to charge to manage the Trust, and also to charge for any legal work he performs. A financial institution can charge to serve as Successor Trustee, and also charge to manage the Trust portfolio.

You could appoint a family member who may serve as Successor Trustee for little or no compensation. But regardless of whether you choose a professional or a family member to be Successor Trustee, you need to come to a written agreement as to what will be charged to manage the Trust. The fee agreement can be included in the Trust document with a provision that whoever accepts the job of Successor Trustee, agrees to accept the fee as provided in the Trust document.

If you do not make written provision for fees, then under Maryland law, the Trustee is entitled to charge a reasonable fee and to charge that fee to the Trust. The Trustee may charge a commission (fee) each year on the value of all of the property held in Trust; as well as on income to the Trust earned on that property. There are statutory guidelines for commissions paid to the Trustee (Est. & Trust 14-103).

ANNUAL COMMISSION ON TRUST PROPERTY

The Trustee is entitled to an annual commission based on the value of Trust property:

.4% on the first $250,000
.25% on the next $250,000
.15% on the next $500,000
.1% on any remaining value

This commission is paid from the Trust property.

ANNUAL COMMISSION ON INCOME TO THE TRUST

The Trustee is also entitled to a commission on income earned by Trust property:

6% on income from real estate, rents and mortgages
6 1/2% on the first $10,000 of all other income
5% on the next $10,000
4% on the next $10,000
3% on any remaining income

The income commission is paid to the Trustee from the Trust income.

The Trustee may employ people to assist with the management of the Trust, such as attorneys, accountants, appraisers, financial planners, etc. (Est. & Trusts 15-102). There are no statutory guidelines for monies paid to the attorney for the Trustee, or any other person employed by the Trustee to administer the Trust.

If a beneficiary of the Trust thinks a fee unreasonable, or that the Trust is being mismanaged, his only recourse is to employ his own attorney and bring the matter before a Court. But the battle is often in favor of the Trustee because he can spend Trust funds to fight the case. And no matter what the outcome, the beneficiary will probably inherit just that much less because of the dispute.

⌧ ☆ THE TRUST IS LEGALLY ENFORCEABLE

Any beneficiary, or Trustee, of the Trust can petition the Court to settle a dispute arising out of the administration of the Trust. If the Trustee is abusing his power or not accounting for Trust funds, the beneficiaries can ask the Court to have the Trustee removed (Est. & Trusts 14-401, 15-112). We gave this section a cross and a star, because the right to have a Trust enforced or administered by a court is a double edged sword. It is great to have a court protect the rights of your beneficiaries, but the cost of a court battle could be greater than if your Estate was subject to Probate in the first place. And as explained, your beneficiaries are at a disadvantage because the Trustee can charge the legal expense of defending his actions to your Trust, but the beneficiaries must pay for the legal battle out of their own pocket.

⌧ PROBATE MIGHT STILL BE NECESSARY

The Trust only works for those items that you place in the Trust. If you have property that is held jointly with another, when you die, that property will go to the joint owner and not to the Trust. If you purchase a security in your name only, and forget to put it in your Trust, a Probate procedure may be necessary to determine who should inherit that security. The attorney who prepares the Trust usually creates a safety net for such a situation by having you sign a "Pour Over Will" at the same time you sign your Trust. The purpose of the Will is to "pour" any asset titled in your name only, into the Trust; specifically, the Will directs your Personal Representative, to put any asset held in your name only, into your Trust. This ensures that all of your property will go to the beneficiaries named in your Trust. But the downside, is that a Probate procedure may be necessary to get the asset into the Trust. You can ensure that no asset will need to be Probated by titling it properly, but the Pour Over Will stands by to clean up any loose ends.

MAYBE PROBATE ISN'T ALL THAT BAD

Although all of the methods discussed in this Chapter can be used to transfer property without the need for Probate, it may be each method has a downside that is objectionable to you. Maybe you don't have enough money to warrant the cost of setting up the Trust at this time. Holding property jointly with another may raise issues of security and independence. Holding property so that it goes directly to a few beneficiaries in a POD, TOD, or ITF account, may not be as flexible as you wish. This is especially the case if you wish to give gifts to several charities or to minor children instead of just one or two beneficiaries. For example, if you hold all your property so that it goes to your son without the need for Probate, and you ask him to use some of the money for your grandchild's education, it may be that your grandchild gets none of the money because your son is sued or falls upon hard times. If you keep your property in your name only and leave a Will giving a certain amount of money for your grandchild, then the child will know exactly how much money you left and the purpose of that gift.

After taking into account all the pros and cons of avoiding Probate, you may well opt for a Will and a Probate procedure. If you make such a decision, it is important to keep in mind that Estate Planning is not an "all or nothing" choice. You can arrange your estate so that certain items pass automatically to your intended beneficiary, and other items can be left in your name only, to be distributed as part of a Probate procedure. By arranging your finances in this manner, you can reduce the value of your Probate estate, and that in turn should reduce the cost of Probate.

Many people decide that the Will is the best route to go but do not act upon it, thinking it unnecessary to prepare a Will until they are very old and about to die. But according to reports published by the National Center for Health Statistics (a division of the U.S. Department of Health and Human Services) 2 of every 10 people who die in any given year are under the age of 60. Twenty percent may seem like a small number until it hits close to home as it did with a young couple. The couple was having difficulty conceiving a child. They went from doctor to doctor until they met someone just beginning his practice. With his knowledge of the latest advances in medicine, he was able to help them. The birth of their child was a moment of joy and gratitude. They asked a nurse to take a picture of them all together — the proud parents, the newborn child and the doctor who made it all possible. Happiness radiated from the picture, but within 6 months, one of them would be dead.

You might think it was the child. An infant's life is so fragile. SIDS and all manner of childhood diseases can threaten a little one. But no, he grew up a healthy young man.

If you looked at the picture, you might guess the husband. Overweight and stressed out; his ruddy complexion suggested high blood pressure. He looked like a typical heart- attack-prone type A personality. No, he was fine and went on to enjoy raising his son.

Probably the wife. She had such a difficult time with the pregnancy and the delivery was especially hard. Perhaps it was all too much for her. No, she recovered and later had two more children.

It was the doctor who was killed in a collision with a truck.

Though we all agree, that one never knows, still people put off making a Will figuring that if they die before getting around to it, Maryland law will take over and their property will be distributed in the manner that they would have wanted anyway. The problem with that logic is the complexity of the Maryland's Laws of Intestate Succession. If you are survived by a spouse, child, parent or sibling, then it isn't too difficult to figure out who will inherit your property. But if none of these survive you, the ultimate beneficiary of your property may not be the person you would have chosen, had you taken the time to do so.

Others think that it is not necessary to have a Will because they have arranged their finances so that all of their property will be inherited without the need for Probate. But money could come into your estate after your death. This could happen in any number of ways from winning the lottery and dying (of happiness, no doubt) to receiving insurance funds after your death. For example, if you die in a house fire or flood the insurance company may need to pay for damage done to your property. In such case, a Personal Representative may need to be appointed and the monies distributed according to Maryland law.

If you die without a Will, the Personal Representative may not be the person you would have chosen. The monies may be distributed differently than you would have wished. And as explained on the next page, there are other important reasons to make a Will.

MAKE GIFTS OF YOUR PERSONAL PROPERTY

Another benefit to making a Will is that you can make provision for who will get your personal property, including your car. If you make a gift of your car in your Will, then it will be relatively simple for your car to be transferred to the beneficiary. If you do not make a specific gift of your car, then it becomes part of your Probate Estate. Your Personal Representative will decide what to do with the car. He can sell it and include the proceeds of the sale in the estate funds to be distributed to your residuary beneficiaries; or he can give the car to one beneficiary of your estate as part of that beneficiary's share of the estate.

SMALL GIFTS MATTER

Many who have lost someone close to them report that the distribution of small personal items caused the greatest conflict. If there is no need for a Probate procedure and the decedent died without a Will, then the next of kin need to decide, among themselves, how personal property is to be distributed. Without guidance from the decedent and no Personal Representative with authority to make decisions, there could be much disagreement and hard feelings, as was the case in the example given on page 127.

CHOOSE A GUARDIAN FOR A MINOR CHILD

Each parent has the right to name someone in their Will to be Guardian of their child in the event that the parent dies before the child is grown, and the other parent is deceased. Should the surviving parent die, then whoever the parent appointed to serve as Guardian can immediately take over the care of the minor child without the need for Court approval (Est. & Trusts 13-701).

MAKE ADJUSTMENT FOR PRIOR GIFTS

You can make adjustments for gifts or loans given during your lifetime. For example, if you have loaned money to a family member and do not expect to be repaid, then you can deduct the loan from that person's inheritance. Of course, it may be that you are not concerned with inequities. That was the case of an aged woman with three children, Paul, Rita and Frank, her youngest. Frank always seemed to need some assist from his mother. She often "lent" him money that he never repaid.

Her other children were responsible and independent. Paul was married and had children of his own. He decided to purchase a house but was having trouble accumulating the down payment. His mother agreed to lend him the money. Paul and his wife offered to give his mother a mortgage on the property. The mother said a simple promissory note from Paul was sufficient, and she would have her attorney draft the note.

The attorney drafted the note but was concerned about the inequity: "You never made a Will. Were you to die, each of your children stands to inherit an equal amount of money. If Paul still owes money on this promissory note, he will either need to pay the balance to your estate, or have it subtracted from the amount he inherits. All of the money you gave to Frank will not count towards his inheritance unless you make a Will saying that amount must be subtracted from his inheritance, or unless Frank gives you a promissory note (Est. & Trusts 3-106).

"It's O.K." replied the woman "I love all my children equally . . . some a little more equal than others."

SET THE PERSONAL REPRESENTATIVE'S FEE

An important reason to make a Will is so that you can choose your Personal Representative and come to an understanding about how much compensation he/she is to receive. You can state that value in your Will.

CAUTION THE PERSONAL REPRESENTATIVE CAN SEEK MORE MONEY

If the amount stated in your Will is less than the statutory value as given on page 144, your Personal Representative may decide to ask the Probate Court to allow the amount as allowed under Maryland statute, or more, if there is some special problem with the Probate procedure. If this is of concern to you, have your attorney draft an agreement with your Personal Representative and attach it to your Will. By signing the Agreement, your Personal Representative is promising to accept the fee as provided in the Will.

Having such a fee agreement cannot prevent your Personal Representative from asking for more money, but with such a document attached to the Will, the Court will not agree to the increase except under extraordinary circumstances.

You also need to keep in mind that the Personal Representative's fee is just to administer the Estate. It does not include payment for professional work he may do while administering the Estate. For example, if you appoint your attorney as Personal Representative, he can agree to the amount stated in the Will for his role as Personal Representative and then ask the Court to award him additional compensation for the performance of his duties as attorney for the Estate.

The same goes for any professional. If you chose an accountant to be your Personal Representative, he can ask to be compensated for his role as Personal Representative and also for any accounting work that he performs while settling the estate. Banks that serve as Personal Representative are entitled to be compensated for their management of the Estate Property in addition to their fee to administer the Estate. If you choose a professional to serve as Personal Representative, then have your compensation agreement also include the amount they will receive to perform their profession duties.

PREPARING YOUR WILL

Some people think that a Will is a simple thing — something they can do themselves. But, it is important to prepare a Will in accordance with the laws of the state of Maryland. If not, then the Will could be challenged, and that may lead to a long, and expensive Court battle. Unless you take the time to make yourself knowledgable about Maryland law as it relates to Wills, it is best to have an attorney who is experienced in Estate Planning, prepare one for you.

STORING THE WILL

Once you sign your Will, you may wonder where to store it. Your attorney may suggest that he place it in his vault for safekeeping. By doing so, he ensures that your heirs will need to contact him as soon as you die. This does not mean that they are required to employ him should a Probate procedure be necessary. It only means that he will have an opportunity for future employment. In exchange, he gives you a good value. Your Will is kept safely in his vault, and at sole cost to him. Should anything happen to that Will, then it is his responsibility to make good the loss.

Before allowing your attorney to store the Will, you should get a receipt and something in writing that says:

- ⇨ The attorney accepts full responsibility for the storage of the Will. Should it be lost or damaged, he will replace the document at no cost to you; and if you are deceased, he will, at no cost to your heirs, present sufficient evidence to the Court to accept a valid copy of the Will into Probate.
- ⇨ There will be no charge to you, or your heirs, for the storage and retrieval of the document.

With all of this cost and liability, many attorneys will agree only to store a copy of your Will. In such case, consider storing your Will with the Register of Wills in the county of your residence for payment of a small fee (currently $5). You are free to retrieve the Will from the Register in the event that you move or decide to change your Will (Est. & Trusts 2-206, 4-201).

Regardless of where you choose to store your Will, let your Personal Representative know that you have a Will and how to retrieve it in the event of your death.

Joint Ownership?
An "In Trust For" account?
A POD Account?
A TOD Security?
A Trust?
A Will?
An Insurance Policy???

This chapter offers so many options that the reader may be more confused than when he was blissfully unenlightened.

As with most things in life, you may find there are no ultimate solutions, just alternatives. The right choice for you is the one that best accomplishes your goal. This being the case, you first need to determine what you want to accomplish with the money you leave. Think about what will happen to your property if you were to die suddenly, without making any plan different from the one you now have.

Who will get your property?
Will any tax need to be paid?
Will Probate be necessary?

If the answers to these questions are not what you wish, then you need to work to retitle your property to accomplish your goals.

For those with significant assets, — especially those with Estates large enough to pay Estate taxes, a trip to an experienced Estate Planning attorney may be well worth the consultation fee.

Continuing To Care 9

There are any number of reasons that people give for wanting to continue on with their lives. For the lucky ones, their main reason for living is that they are having a great time and don't want it to end. For many, it is a more a sense of responsibility. During child rearing years the concern of the parent is what will happen to the child should the parent suddenly die. Once a child is grown, the roles often reverse, and it is the child worrying about what will happen to his parent if the child were not present to see to the care of the aging parent. Even pet lovers worry about what will happen to their pet should the owner no longer be around.

There is little that can be done to prepare those who depend on you for the loss of your companionship and emotional support; but there are many things you can do to provide financial support for those who rely on you. Even people of modest means can make financial provision so their loved ones will have an easy transition from being dependent to becoming self sufficient.

This chapter explains the many simple, and relatively inexpensive, things you can do to provide care for your loved ones should you not be present to do so yourself.

It doesn't happen very often, but both parents could die or become incapacitated before their child reaches adulthood. Most parents don't want to think about, much-less prepare for such a happening. But in this age of postponing parenthood, many parents are raising children into their fifties and sixties. The probability of a life threatening illness increases with age, so parents need to understand the importance of planning ahead.

Regardless of the parent's age, planning for the care of a minor child should be part of every parent's Estate Plan, not only because it is the responsible thing to do, but also because it is relatively simple and inexpensive to do.

A child must be cared for in two ways, the ***person*** of the child and the ***property*** of the child. To care for the person of the child, someone must be in charge of the child's everyday living, not only food and shelter but to provide social, ethical and religious training. Someone must have legal authority to make medical decisions and see to the child's education.

To care for the child's property, someone must be responsible to see that monies left to the child are used for the care of the child and that anything left over is preserved until the child becomes an adult.

If one parent dies, then it is the right, and duty, of the surviving parent to care for the child. But it could happen that both parents become incapacitated or die before the child is grown. Each parent can name someone in their Will to serve as Guardian of their minor child (Est. & Trusts 13-701).

It would be nice if both parents name the same person in their respective Wills to be Guardian, but the reality is that parents often disagree about who is best qualified to raise the child. In such case, the Will of the last parent to die controls. Should the last surviving parent die, the person appointed as Guardian can immediately take over the care of the minor child, without seeking Court approval.

APPOINTING A STANDBY GUARDIAN

A parent can appoint a ***Standby Guardian*** who will assume the care of a minor child in the event that both parents are unable to care for the child. For example, if one parent is deceased and the surviving parent becomes ill with a debilitating disease, the surviving parent can appoint someone to take over the care for his/her minor child should the surviving parent become incapacitated. The appointment of a Standby Guardian is easily done by signing the statutory form of the DESIGNATION OF STANDBY GUARDIAN. The form can be downloaded from the Internet (see page X of the Introduction) or found in any law library. Appointing a Standby Guardian does not change the right of the parent to care for the child. The parent is free to revoke the Designation at any time (Est. & Trusts 13-904, 13-907).

PROVIDING FOR THE CHILD'S SUPPORT

As any parent is well aware, it is expensive to raise a child. People that you might consider to be the best choice to serve as your child's Guardian might not be able to do so unless you leave sufficient monies to pay for the care of the child. If you are a person of limited finances, then consider purchasing a term life insurance policy on your life and/or on the life of the other parent of the child. If you can only afford one policy, then insure the life of the parent who contributes most to the support of the child.

Term insurance policies are relatively inexpensive if you limit the term to just that period of time until your child becomes an adult. Some companies offer a combination of term life and disability insurance. As with any other purchase, it is important to comparison shop to obtain the best price for the coverage. If you are married, you may want to name your spouse as the beneficiary of the term insurance policy with your child as an alternate beneficiary.

Married or single, you can name your child as the primary beneficiary of the policy. But as explained on page 176, if the insurance funds exceed $5,000, the insurance company will require Court authorization before transferring the insurance proceeds. The Court will probably appoint a Guardian to care for the property until the child reaches 18. If the surviving parent is able to care for the child, then the Court will appoint the parent as Guardian of the child's property. Regardless of who is appointed as Guardian, the Court will supervise the guardianship and require the Guardian to account to the Court on a regular basis .

Guardianship procedures are expensive to set up and maintain. The Court may require the Guardian to be bonded, and that cost is charged to the property inherited by the child. The Guardian will need to be represented by an attorney, and the attorney's fees will be charged to the child's property.

If the surviving parent can care for the person of the child, then it is important to avoid having a Guardianship established for property that you may leave to the child. One solution is to set up a Trust for the child, but if you have limited finances then a good alternative is to appoint someone to serve as Custodian of the gift under the Maryland Uniform Transfers to Minors Act. That law is explained on the next page.

If you wish to leave property to a child, then you can appoint someone to be the Custodian of the gift under the Maryland Uniform Transfers To Minors Act. This law is designed to protect gifts made to a minor. The Custodian can be a trusted friend or relative, or you can name a bank or other financial institution to serve as Custodian. It is appropriate to use the Uniform Transfers To Minors Act if you want to make the child a beneficiary of your Will or of a life insurance policy, or even of a bank account. For example, you can name the bank as Custodian of the bank account in the event that you die before the child reaches the age of 21:

> RUSSELL JONES POD FRIENDLY BANK as Custodian For RUSSELL JONES, JR under the Maryland Uniform Transfers to Minors Act.

The gift does not become effective until you die. During your lifetime you are free to add to or subtract from the account. You can close the account or change beneficiaries, or even appoint someone else to serve as Custodian of the property. Should you die after the child reaches 21, the bank will give the balance of the account to your beneficiary. If you die before the child is 21, the bank will hold and manage the account as directed by Maryland statute. Under Maryland law, the Custodian has the discretion to use the funds for the care of the child. The Custodian can pay monies directly to the child, or use the money for the child's benefit. The Custodian can refuse to use any of the monies for the child and just keep the funds invested. A family member, or even the child once he is 14, can ask the Probate Court to order the Custodian to part with some or all of the money. The Judge will decide what is in the child's best interest and then rule on the matter (Est. & Trusts 13-303, 13-314, 13-320).

A gift made under the Maryland Uniform Transfers to Minors Act can be made to one child only and only one person or company can serve as Custodian. If you wish to make a gift to two children, then you will need to make a separate gift to each of them (Est. & Trusts 13-310).

You can use the Maryland Uniform Transfers to Minors Act to make a gift to a minor under your Will. You can name someone to be Custodian to care for a gift until the child reaches 21. If you die after the child has reached the specified age, your Personal Representative will give the gift directly to the child. If the child has not reached the specified age, the Personal Representative will give the gift to the Custodian to hold and manage for the benefit of the child (Est. & Trusts 13-305).

The Custodian is required by law to invest and manage the property in a responsible, prudent manner. He is entitled to be paid for his effort (Est. & Trusts 13-315). If your gift is sizeable, then the Custodian's fee can be sizeable. Before appointing a person or a company as Custodian, it is best to come to a written agreement about what will be charged to manage the custodial property.

☎ LAWYER   A TRUST FOR THE CHILD

If you have sufficient monies to care for your child until adulthood, then consult with an attorney about setting up a Trust for the child or drafting a Will with a Trust provision in the event you die before the child is grown. The only problem with having a Trust included in your Will is that the Trust is funded by your Probate Estate. If you have a significant amount of money, the better route might be to set up a Revocable Living Trust. You can fund the Trust while you are alive and bypass Probate altogether.

The person you name as Trustee will handle the Trust funds should you die before the child reaches maturity. You can name the other parent as your Trustee, or if you wish, you can appoint a financial institution to manage the Trust funds. If you do not appoint the other parent as Trustee, then that parent still has the right, and duty, to provide for the child. If you instruct the Trustee to use Trust funds for the child's support and maintenance, then the Trustee can set up a payment schedule with the child's parent to use the funds for everyday necessities.

If you instruct the Trustee to keep all of the funds invested until the child reaches maturity, then the Trustee will do so and distribute the Trust funds directly to the child at whatever age you specify in the Trust document.

PROVIDING FOR THE STEPCHILD

Perhaps the reason that the story of Cinderella has such universal appeal is that many stepchildren, at one point or another, feel left out. The law seems to reinforce that perception. Unless your spouse provides otherwise, you, and not your stepchild, have the right to make health care decisions for your spouse in the event of his/her incapacity (Health-Gen. 5-605). And if all of your spouse's property is held jointly with you, then should your spouse die first, your stepchild will be left nothing.

Of course giving you the right to inherit all of your spouse's estate must be a decision that is agreeable to your spouse. If your spouse wants your step-child to inherit property, then your spouse can arrange his/her finances so that the child will inherit property. Hopefully, your spouse will consult with an estate planning attorney who can explain the best way to achieve that goal, else that intent could be thwarted and the child end up with less than your spouse intended as was the case in the example given on page 121.

Also, your spouse has the choice of giving your stepchild the right to make medical decisions by signing an Advance Directive that appoints the child as Health Care Agent for your spouse. And your spouse can sign a Power of Attorney giving your stepchild power to manage your spouse's finances in the event that your spouse is unable to do so (see Page 233).

The stepparent often comes across as villain, but it is the parent, and not the stepparent, who decides whether to allow the child's input on medical and financial decisions. And it is the parent, not the stepparent, who decides whether the child shall inherit property belonging to the parent.

THE SECOND MARRIAGE TRUST

A relatively simple solution to the problem of providing for children of a prior marriage is to have a Trust prepared. If you have minor children from a prior marriage, your can have a Trust prepared that will provide funds to care for the children till grown, and at that time, the monies be distributed to your surviving spouse and children in whatever manner you wish. If your children are grown, you may want the income of the Trust to be used to support your surviving spouse; and once the spouse dies, the remainder distributed to your children. A properly drafted Trust can provide for the care of your spouse and child in what ever way you think best.

That was the case with an elderly widower who married a pretty girl one quarter of his age. Their Pre-nuptial Agreement made it clear that all his property would go to his son from his first marriage. Surprisingly, the marriage turned out well. So well that the couple had two daughters. The husband decided to divide his estate equally between his three children and to provide for the care of his wife until the youngest child was grown.

His attorney suggested a Trust. "You can be Trustee during your lifetime. Once you die, your successor Trustee can immediately distribute one-third of the Trust to your son who is now 55. No sense to keep him waiting. The rest of your money can remain in your Trust. Income from the Trust can be used to support your wife and children until the youngest is 25. Then, whatever remains in the Trust can be distributed equally to your daughters.".

"Good idea" said the elderly gentlemen, with a smile "Just make sure it is revocable during my lifetime. Who knows what adventures I might be up to in the future?"

PROVIDING FOR THE ADULT CHILD

It isn't just stepchildren who can be left out if no provision is made. Even children from a long-standing marriage can be cut off against the wishes of a parent. A parent may assume that all of their children will be treated equally once both parents are gone, but if all of their property is held jointly, the last parent to die is the one who gets to decide "who gets what." Too often, the wishes of the deceased parent are ignored, for example:

THE STRAINED RELATIONSHIP: A child may have a close relationship with one parent, and a strained, but tolerable, relationship with the other. Peace in the family is achieved because the parent who is close to the child acts as a buffer. Should the buffer parent die first, the relationship between the surviving parent and the child may fall apart altogether and the child's inheritance be cut off.

THE PARENT WITH DIMINISHED CAPACITY: The more common scenario, is that the surviving parent becomes increasingly dependent on one child — either for emotional support, or for physical assistance as the parent ages. The other children may live at a distance, or perhaps they are too involved with their own family to assist. The supporting child may end up with most, if not all, of what was intended for all of the children.

These problems can be avoided by having your attorney prepare a Family Trust. The family assets are placed in the Trust with the parents as co-Trustees. The beneficiaries of the Trust cannot be changed unless both parents agree to the change. Once one parent dies, the Trust becomes irrevocable. The Trust income goes to the surviving parent and once that parent dies, whatever remains in the Trust is distributed in the manner as was agreed by both parents.

CARING FOR THE CARETAKER

If you are the caretaker of someone who is incapacitated, then in addition to preparing your own estate plan, you need to be concerned about who will care for the incapacitated person should something happen to you. Someone will need to make medical decisions for the incapacitated person and see to it that he/she is properly housed and fed.

APPOINTMENT OF A SUCCESSOR CARETAKER

Often a family member will agree to take responsibility for the care of an incapacitated person in the event that the caretaker dies. But perhaps no one wants the job, or the opposite case, too many want to have control. For example, if a parent is incapacitated, one child may want the parent to remain at home with the assistance of a home health care worker. Another child may think the best place for the parent is an assisted living facility with 24 hour care. The caretaker spouse may be concerned that a tug-of-war will erupt once he dies.

In such case, the caretaker spouse should consult with an attorney to ensure future care for the incapacitated spouse. The attorney may suggest that a Guardian be appointed for the incapacitated spouse while the caretaker is alive. The Court can appoint a Co-Guardian, who can take over the job should the caretaker spouse be unable to continue. Once the Guardianship is in place, the court will continue to supervise the care of the incapacitated person until he/she is restored to capacity or dies (Est. & Trusts 13-220, 13-705).

☎ LAWYER

A SPECIAL NEEDS TRUST FOR THE INCAPACITATED

If a person is incapacitated, both the federal and state government provide assistance with programs such as Social Security disability benefits and custodial nursing home care under the Medicaid program. The family often supplements the government program by providing for the incapacitated person's ***special needs***, such as clothing, hobbies, special education, outings to a movie or a sports event — things that give the incapacitated person some quality of life.

To be eligible for government assistance programs the incapacitated must be essentially without funds. Caretakers fear that leaving money to the incapacitated in a Will or Trust will disqualify the incapacitated from further government assistance. Understanding this dilemma, the federal government allow a parent, grandparent or legal guardian to set up a ***Medicaid Special Needs Trust*** as authorized by 42 U.S.C. 1396(d)(4) with the incapacitated as the beneficiary of the Trust.

The statute allows the Trustee to use Trust funds to provide for the special needs of the incapacitated. If any funds remain in the Special Needs Trust after the incapacitated dies, then those monies must be used to reimburse the state for monies spent on behalf of the incapacitated person.

An experienced Elder Law attorney can explain the different options available to the family to continue to provide for the incapacitated person's special needs in the event that the caretaker family member dies.

CARING FOR YOUR PET

A woman died at peace,
leaving her fortune
and care of her cat to her niece.
Alas, the fortune and the cat
Soon disappeared after that.

You could leave money to someone with the understanding that the person will take care of your pet, but the moral of the above limerick, is that just leaving money will not guarantee care for your pet.

☎ LAWYER TRUST FOR CARE OF PET

If you are financially able, you can employ an attorney to set up a Trust for the care of your pet, or you can have the attorney include a Trust provision in your Will. The person you name as Trustee will be charged with the duty to use the Trust funds to pay for the care of the pet. You should also name a remainder beneficiary (a person or charitable organization) to receive whatever remains in the Trust after the pet dies.

If you intend the Trustee to also serve as custodian of your pet, then you can ask the remainder beneficiary to regularly check to see that the pet is treated humanely, if not benevolently.

If you don't have the resources to set up a Trust to care for your pet, you can still ask a fellow pet lover to care for the animal. If no one among your circle of family and friends is able to do so, then ask your pet's veterinarian to consider starting an "Orphaned Pet Service" to assist in finding new homes for pets who lose their owners. It is good public relations and a potential source of income. If this is agreeable to the Veterinarian, you can make arrangements in your Will to pay the Vet to care for the pet until a suitable family can be found. This is a more humane approach than the, all too common practice, of putting a pet "to sleep" rather than have the pet suffer the loss of its master. And in at least one case, that reasoning backfired.

Eleanor always had a pet in the house. After her husband died, her two poodles were her constant companions. When Eleanor became ill with cancer, she worried about what would happen to her "buddies" if she died. She finally decided it best to have her family put them to sleep when she died.

Eleanor endured surgery, chemotherapy, radiation therapy, and even some holistic remedies, but she continued to go downhill. Eleanor's family came in to visit her at the hospital to say their last good-byes. She was so ill, she didn't even recognize them. No one thought she could last the day. Because the family was from out of state, and time short, they decided to put the pets to sleep so they need only take care of the funeral arrangements when she died.

To everyone's surprise, Eleanor rallied. She lived two more long, lonely years.

She often said she wished they had put her to sleep instead of her buddies.

ARRANGING TO PAY BILLS

When people think about their Estate Plan they are more concerned about giving their possessions away than thinking about paying bills. If you are the breadwinner of the family, then you need to think about how your family will manage without you. Eventually, all who are dependent on you will need to fend for themselves, but there are things you can do to help them through the transition period until they become self sufficient.

First and foremost is to consider how monies you owe will be paid. If you don't give this some serious thought, then your Estate could be quickly depleted. Even people who have no dependents need to give this some thought. If not, then all the heirs may inherit is a bunch of unpaid bills. This was the case with Larry. He had no family to speak of. After his wife died, he bought a condominium in Rockville, Maryland. Over the years, he developed a close network of friends. They became his family. Larry did not have much money. He had a mortgage on the condominium. His car was leased. But he wanted his friends to know how much they meant to him so he had a Will drafted giving all he owned to five close friends.

The friends appreciated the gesture but the inheritance turned out to be a nightmare. They had to keep current the mortgage payments and the maintenance fees until the condominium was sold. Because Larry left little cash, this money had to come out of the beneficiaries' pockets. Two were living on their Social Security income and they had to borrow money from the others to contribute to their share of the upkeep.

The beneficiaries had no money to settle the lease on the car. Even if they did, they decided that there was no point in doing so because the amount needed to obtain clear title was greater than the current market value of the car. The beneficiaries decided not to make any further payment and they returned the car to the leasing agent. Their decision turned out to be a losing proposition. The leasing agent took the car, sold it and then sued the estate for the balance of the monies owed on the lease.

Because the beneficiaries had to quickly liquidate the estate, the condominium sold for less than it would have had they the time, energy and resources to fix it up. After they settled with the leasing agent, paid off the funeral expenses, mortgage, and Probate fees there was only a few hundred dollars left. That was a lot of work and stress for nothing.

The pity was that Larry could have arranged his finances so that his beneficiaries were not burdened by his debt. He could have taken out mortgage insurance as part of the loan package. In most cases the cost of the insurance is nominal and is included as part of the monthly mortgage payment.

Larry could have done the same when he leased the car. Most leasing contracts offer term life insurance as an option. The cost of such insurance depends on the age of the person, the term of the loan and the amount of monies owed, but the premium paid each month is just a small fraction of the loan payment.

Even if Larry just arranged for payment of one of these debts, his beneficiaries would have come away with the gift that Larry intended, instead of the headache that they inherited.

PROVIDE FOR CREDIT CARD DEBT

If you have significant credit card debt, you need to consider how that debt will be paid once you die. Most credit card companies offer insurance policies and include the premium as part of your monthly payment. If you have such insurance, then should you die, any outstanding balance is paid. It benefits the credit card company to offer life insurance as part of the credit package, because they are assured of prompt payment should the borrower die. However, if you have little or no assets and no one other than yourself is liable to pay the debt, you may have no incentive to pay for insurance that can only benefit the lender.

As discussed in Chapters 2 and 4, if you hold a credit card jointly with another person, both of you are equally liable to pay the debt. If one of you dies, the other is responsible to pay the bill regardless of who ran up the bill. If paying that bill might be a struggle for the surviving debtor, then the better route to go is for each of you to have your own credit card.

Still another reason not to hold a joint credit card is that each of you can establish your own line of credit. This is especially important if you are married and one of you is retired or has been out of the job market for any period of time. Should the breadwinner die, it may be difficult for the surviving partner to establish credit if he/she has no recent work record It is easier for the unemployed spouse to establish a line of credit when he/she is married to someone who is working.

The good part of purchasing loan insurance — be it credit card insurance, mortgage insurance or car insurance, is that you can usually purchase the insurance without taking a medical examination. The down side is that such insurance may be more expensive than a life insurance policy. If you are in fairly good health, consider taking out a life insurance policy to cover all of your outstanding loans. The cost of the single life insurance policy may be significantly less than purchasing separate loan insurance policies.

The Estate Planning strategy of purchasing life insurance to pay off all of your loans works best by making your Probate Estate the beneficiary of the policy and then directing the Executor of your Will to use those proceeds to pay your policy. If you are married and your spouse is jointly liable for your debts, you can name your spouse as the beneficiary of the insurance proceeds. Your spouse can use that money to pay off all of the joint debts.

If you name your spouse, child or family member who is dependent on you for support, as the beneficiary of the insurance proceeds and that person has no legal obligation to pay your debts, then none of your creditors can force your family member to use any part of those funds to pay your debts (Est. & Trusts 8-115, Insur. 16-111). If you want to be sure that your spouse, child or dependent family member receives money after you are gone, and you do not want those funds used to pay off your debts, then this strategy should accomplish your goal.

With or without debt, you may be wondering about life insurance — should you have it? How much is enough? The answer to these questions depends on the "sleep at night" factor, namely how much insurance do you need to make you not worry about insurance coverage when you go to sleep at night? It is often more an emotional than a financial issue.

Some people have an "every man for himself" attitude and are content to have no life insurance at all. When they die, whatever they have, they have. And that is what their heirs will inherit. Others worry about how their loved ones will manage if they are not around to support them, and decide to purchase enough insurance to maintain their dependents in their accustomed life style.

The same person may have different thoughts about insurance coverage as the circumstances of their life changes — from no coverage in their bachelor days to more-than-enough coverage in their child rearing days to just-enough-to-bury-me in their senior years.

Insurance companies recognize that people's needs change over the years. Many companies offer flexible insurance coverage. As with any consumer item, it is a good idea to shop around.

Special Situation

PROVIDING FOR THE FAMILY BUSINESS

If you own a business, you need to think about to what will happen to that business in the event of your incapacity or death. Do you want the person who inherits the business to take over its daily operations or do you think it best to have the business sold and have the proceeds of the sale given to your beneficiaries? If you do not make provision for the orderly transfer of your business, then the Probate Court may need to make that decision for you. If you own a sole proprietorship, your Personal Representative can continue to operate that business for 4 months. That time period can be extended by Court order (Est. & Trust 7-401).

In addition to the running of the business you need to consider how company debts will be paid. If your business is highly leveraged (business talk for "owes lots of money"), you also need to consider how those loans will be paid should you become disabled or die. Taxes are still another concern. Your business may be worth millions on paper, and your Estate taxes based on that value. You heirs may be forced to sell the company just to pay the taxes, but without your leadership they may get only a fraction of the value of the company. A solution to the problem is to purchase a key man or life insurance policy to pay taxes and get the company through the transition period. An attorney or a financial planner who is experienced in business matters can offer other suggestions as to the best method of ensuring that the business continues its operation, or terminates in an orderly fashion — whichever is applicable in your case.

ESTATE PLANNING FOR THE BANKRUPT

You may think the above title to be an oxymoron (a contradiction in terms). If a person is bankrupt, why plan for an estate he doesn't have? But facts are, that people who file for bankruptcy are often quite wealthy and that is their downfall. Because they have substantial income or property, banks and people are willing to lend them money. If more money is borrowed than can be repaid, the unhappy result is bankruptcy. In the event that you are concerned about meeting your responsibilities as parent or spouse, yet you enjoy a life style of financial brinkmanship, then consider investing in items that are "creditor proof."

That's exactly what Alan decided to do. Alan was an astute man, well aware of his strengths and weaknesses. He was a sharp businessman, someone who enjoyed his work and who knew he had the capacity to earn large sums of money. But he also knew he was a gambler. Not the Las Vegas type, but a gambler in business ventures. "No risk, no gain" was his favorite saying.

If you charted his net worth over the years it would look like the peaks and valleys of the NASDAQ. Lots of high highs and lots of low lows. Unfortunately, he married a woman who did not share his adventurous spirit. His wife became increasingly intolerant of their financial instability. She came to realize that this was his life style and things would never change. "All gamblers die broke," she said as she walked out the door with their 5 year old daughter in tow.

That, and the fact that he had to declare bankruptcy, brought Alan up short; and he began to be concerned about his future and that of his family.

Alan talked things over with his bankruptcy attorney "I am a good businessman, but not a clairvoyant. There was no way to predict the turn of events that led to this situation. But I know I will bounce back, and it will just be a matter of time before I am earning a good living. I also know that I am an entrepreneur and not a 9 to 5 type guy so this could happen again. What concerns me is how to provide some security for my child in the event that something happens to me before she is grown." His attorney's response was a surprise:
"Move to another state."

"You're kidding."

"Not really. There are few items in Virginia that are creditor proof. You could set up a pension plan and your daughter could inherit those funds free from the claims of your creditors "(Courts & Jud. Proc. 11-504).

Alan didn't think that would work. "I am my own boss, and I don't have the self discipline to put money aside each month for my retirement."

The attorney suggested "You could purchase a life insurance policy and make her the beneficiary of the policy. You might even consider setting up an annuity for your daughter so that she will have a steady income through her school years (Est. & Trusts 8-115, Insur. 16-111). She can inherit the money free of your creditors. The only problem, is that if you get into serious financial difficulties, during your lifetime your creditors could force you to cash in the policy to pay your debt. There is a way around the problem by setting up an Irrevocable Insurance Trust. When you are ready to do some serious Estate Planning, we can get together and discuss Irrevocable Trusts and other sophisticated Estate Planning strategies."

ANNUITIES TO SPREAD THE INHERITANCE

It is not uncommon for an heir go through his inheritance within two years. For many, the reason the money is gone so soon, is that there just wasn't much money to inherit in the first place. But for others, it's a spending frenzy. You probably know your heirs well enough to know whether they are squirrels, always saving for the winter or whether it is their life style to Earn-A-Penny Spend-A-Penny.

If you want to leave an insurance policy benefit to someone you love, but the intended beneficiary is immature, or a born spendthrift, then a simple solution to the problem may be to purchase an annuity rather than life insurance. An annuity is a type of insurance policy that can be set up so that your beneficiary (the ***annuitant***) receives money on a monthly, or yearly basis, rather than a single lump sum payment when you die. There are different kinds of annuities, so again, it is important to shop around.

An annuity can also be set up to benefit your favorite charity, and to reduce, if not eliminate the Capital Gains Tax. For example, suppose you own several acres of land in West Virginia that you purchased many years ago. You may have been putting off selling the property because of the Capital Gains Tax. But it has been a liability to you. It produces no income and because the property continues to appreciate, each year, you are paying more and more in property taxes. If you are living on a pension income, it makes no sense to continue to pay money in property taxes, when that money could be used to give you additional income. A solution to the problem may be to donate the property to your favorite charity with an agreement that they will sell the property and use the money to purchase an annuity that will give you an income for your life. The agreement is called the ***Charitable Remainder Annuity Trust***.

A Charitable Remainder Annuity Trust is a Trust that is established according to the Internal Revenue Code (IRC 664). Charities do not pay taxes, so property donated to the Trust can be sold by the Trustee free of the Capital Gains Tax. The money from the sale is invested so that it provides an income (an annuity) to you either for a fixed period of time, say 20 years, or for your lifetime as computed by actuarial tables (i.e., your estimated life expectancy). It can even be set up so that the annuity continues to be paid to your spouse after your death.

How much income you receive and how much goes to the charity, depends on several factors, including the value of the donated property and the length of time the annuity is paid. Your financial planner or Estate Planning attorney can suggest the type of Charitable Trust that best meets your Estate Planning goals.

Of course there is always the downside and Charitable Remainder Annuity Trust is no exception. It may cost significant attorney fees to set up the Trust. Some charities may offer to have their attorney prepare the Trust at no cost to you, or perhaps they offer a "standard" Trust document that their attorney prepared. But using their Trust document represents a conflict of interest. Their Trust was prepared by an attorney for the greatest benefit to his client (that's the charity, not you). It is important that you employ your own attorney to represent you. He knows the extent of your Estate and he understands what you wish to accomplish. Once established, the Trust is irrevocable, so it is important that you understand all of the aspects of the Trust, including what income taxes you will need to pay on the annuity that you receive.

If you decide to set up a Charitable Remainder Annuity Trust, then the benefits to you are many:

☑ TAX SAVINGS

Had you sold the property and invested the money yourself, you would have had to pay a Capital Gains Tax and that tax could be substantial, depending on the tax rate in effect at the time of the transfer. By gifting the property the full value of the land can be used to produce investment income.

You will no longer need to pay annual property taxes. And you even get to take a charitable deduction on your income tax return in the year the gift is made.

☑ NO PROBATE EXPENSE

Because the land is in a different state, it could be both time consuming and expensive to transfer the property to your beneficiaries upon your death. By donating the property to the Trust, you avoid the need for a Probate procedure in another state.

☑ CREDITOR PROTECTION

If you keep the land and are sued, you could lose it to pay your creditors. If your spouse inherited the land, it could be lost to creditors. But once the property is transferred into the Trust, the gift is made. Neither your creditors nor the creditors of any successor annuitant of the Trust can get access to the Trust property. The most the creditor can do is ask for payment from the money received as an income.

☑ SPENDTHRIFT PROVISION

If your spouse is a spendthrift and inherited the land, all of the money could be spent in short order. You can set up this annuity Trust for the benefit of your spouse and be assured that your spouse will have a steady income over a long period of time.

☑ GIVE WHEN NEEDED INSTEAD OF LATER

A Charitable Remainder Annuity Trust can be set up in any number of different ways to accommodate your Estate Plan. For example, if you are not in need of a present income, but expect that you will spend significant sums on your child's education, you can set up a 20 year annuity with your child as the annuitant. This will get the child through college and probably be a great help in should the child decide to start a family. Why have the child inherit property in later, high earning years rather than in the early, high expense/low income years?

☑ GOOD DEED

If you are concerned that you will be paying a significant Capital Gains Tax, it means that your property has appreciated significantly, and you are fortunate indeed. By setting up a Charitable Remainder Annuity Trust, you are making a donation to the charity of your choice because whatever is left in the Trust after the annuity is paid, goes to the charity. By setting up a Charitable Trust, you are sharing your good fortune with others. You can consider this as "giving back" to the community, or just plain doing a good deed.

A Health Care Estate Plan 10

The last two chapters discussed the distribution or management of your estate once you are deceased. But in this age of an extended life expectancy, a more important topic is how to manage and preserve your estate in the event of a debilitating illness. As life expectancy increases, so does the percentage of the population who suffer incapacity from debilitating strokes, Alzheimer's disease or Parkinsons' disease. It is estimated that more than 50% of the population who are 85 or older, suffer some degree of dementia. Your best estate plan could be sabotaged by lengthy or incapacitating illness.

A ***Health Care Estate Plan*** is a plan designed to care for your person and property in the event of an incapacitating illness. In Chapter 7 we discussed how you can appoint Health Care Agent to make your medical decisions in the event that you are too ill to do so yourself. Your Health Care Agent will care for your person in the event of your incapacity. But there is still the problem of who will care for your property.

In this chapter we will discuss how you can appoint someone to handle your finances in the event of your incapacity, and how you can arrange to pay for the health care that you may require as you age.

A TRUST TO CARE FOR PROPERTY

The optimum way to provide for the care of your property in the event of your incapacity, is to set up a Trust appointing a Successor Trustee to care for your property according to the directions given in your Trust. You can be Trustee of the funds while you have capacity. Should you become incapacitated, then the person you name as Successor Trustee will take over. If you are a person of substance, then you should consider having an attorney design a Trust especially for you.

You may be wondering what we mean by the term "a person of substance." We have avoided defining the term because wealth is a state of mind. If you think back on your life, you can probably recall times of well being, where you felt on top of the world and a fortunate person. Excluding winners of game shows and the lottery, for most of us, the moment we felt most wealthy did not coincide with the high point of our net worth. Except for the extremes of abject poverty and Bill Gates, whether you are poor or wealthy depends more on your subjective perception than any objective standard. Using this subjective standard, you should have a Trust prepared when you feel rich enough to conclude that the benefits of a Trust justify the cost of preparing and maintaining the Trust.

And just to keep things grounded in reality, take an objective view of your finances by determining your ***Net Worth*** (the cash value of your assets, less the amount of monies you owe). You can use the form on the next page to calculate that value. If you are married and hold all property jointly, then calculate the Net Worth of all of the assets and divide by 2, for your own Net Worth.

DETERMINING YOUR NET WORTH

ASSETS:

$ ________________ Cash (coin collection, bank accounts, certificates of deposit, etc.)

$________________ Cash value of insurance policies

$ ________________ Securities (stocks, bonds, mutuals, etc.)

$________________ Pension Plans, IRA's, etc.

$________________ Cash value of a partnership or other business interest

$________________ Tangible personal property (jewelry, private art or stamp collections, motor vehicles, etc.)

$________________ Real property (residences, vacant lots, condominiums, cooperatives, time shares, etc.)

$________________ TOTAL VALUE OF ASSETS

It may be that you and the bank own all of this, so you need to subtract away monies that you owe on any of the above items:

LIABILITIES

$________________ Private loans

$________________ Mortgage Balance

$________________ Credit card debt

$________________ Car loan or car lease balance

$________________ TOTAL LIABILITIES

A simple subtraction gives you your ***net worth***:

ASSETS — LIABILITIES = NET WORTH

THE CONVENIENCE ACCOUNT

If you do not have sufficient assets to justify the cost of employing an attorney to draft a Trust, and you are concerned that at some time in the future you may become incapacitated and unable to handle your finances, then there are strategies, other than a Trust, that you can use to solve the problem.

You can set up a joint checking account so that a trusted family member can write checks on the account. Of course there are all the inherent problems of a joint account that we discussed on page 173. You can avoid many of those problems by limiting the amount of money that can be accessed by the family member. For example, you can arrange your finances so that all of your bills are paid from a single checking account and your family member can access that account, only.

If you set up a joint account, your family member will own whatever is in the account should your die. If this is not as you wish, you can set up a ***Convenience Account*** authorizing a family member to write checks on your account (Finan. Inst. 1-204). You can instruct the bank that in the event of your death the family member may no longer access your account. But ultimately the family member must be trustworthy because the bank is under no duty to stop your family member from writing checks on your account until the bank learns of your death.

AVOIDING GUARDIANSHIP

The joint or convenience account solves the problem of how to pay your bills in the event you are temporarily ill. It does not solve the problem of how to manage your business affairs in the event of an extended illness. For example, suppose you have a stroke and can no longer be cared for at home. Should it be necessary for you to sell your home and move to an assisted living facility, then no one will have the authority to sell the house for you. In such case, the Court will need to appoint a Guardian to transact business on your behalf, and probably to make your medical decisions as well.

The person appointed as your Guardian is entitled to be paid for his services. The amount paid for the Guardian of your property is the same as the statutory amount for the compensation of Trustees. See page 189 for the schedule of fees (Est. & Trusts 13-218).

The duties of a Guardian are the same as those of a Personal Representative. He must take possession of your assets, file an inventory with the Court, and each year, account to the Court for monies spent. The Court may decide that a bond is necessary for the protection of your assets (Est. & Trusts 13-208, 13-209).

As with a Personal Representative, the Guardian needs to employ an attorney to establish guardianship and then see to it that it is properly administered. Attorney's fees must be approved by the Court. The hourly rate is much the same as the Court awards to attorneys to administer a Probate Estate. Court filing fees, the cost of a bond, attorney's fees, Guardian fees, all are paid from your estate (that's your money!).

Guardianship procedures are expensive to set up and maintain. Curious that so many people worry about how to avoid Probate, when the larger concern should be how to avoid Guardianship proceedings. Consider that it is not all that hard to arrange your finances so that no Probate is necessary. The cost to administer your estate should be $0. Even with a full Probate procedure, the administration usually ends within a year.

Whatever it costs to Probate your estate is a one-time expense. Once monies are distributed to the beneficiaries, it is ended. Not so if you become incapacitated. It can cost thousands of dollars to set up the guardianship. Once established the Guardian and his attorney are entitled to reasonable fees. And this expense continues until you are returned to capacity, or die.

One way to avoid the need to have a Court appoint a Guardian of your person is to sign an Advance Directive appointing someone to be your Health Care Agent (see page 166). Should you become physically incapacitated, your Health Care Agent can make your medical decisions.

You can appoint someone to handle your financial affairs in the event that you are too ill to do so your self. A Trust is the best vehicle because you can place all of your assets into a Trust and have your Successor Trustee take over in the event of your incapacity. For those of limited means, a Power of Attorney is the next best Estate Plan.

A POWER OF ATTORNEY FOR FINANCES

A Durable Power of Attorney is a document by which someone (the ***Principal***) gives another (his ***Attorney-In-Fact*** or ***Agent***) authority to do certain acts on behalf of the Principal. The word ***durable*** refers to the fact that Power of Attorney continues to remain in effect even though the Principal may later become incapacitated (Est. & Trusts 13-601).

You can give your Attorney-In-Fact general powers to manage your finances, to do much the same with your property as you can do yourself, such as:

- ➪ sell any of your real or personal property;
- ➪ buy real or personal property for you;
- ➪ trade in securities;
- ➪ pay your bills and/or taxes;
- ➪ operate your business;
- ➪ have access to your safe deposit box;
- ➪ borrow money on your behalf;
- ➪ purchase insurance policies and name beneficiaries;
- ➪ sue or defend a law suit on your behalf.

You can even give your Attorney-In-Fact power to make gifts of your property in accordance with your estate plan, for example, you can direct him to give certain family members up to $10,000 in gifts each year.

Instead of giving your Attorney-In-Fact broad general powers, you can limit the things he can do with your property to just one or two things that you authorize in your Power of Attorney.

Limited or general, the operative word in any Power of Attorney is POWER. Once your Attorney-In-Fact has authority to act, he essentially steps in your shoes and can do whatever you gave him authority to do. Your primary consideration in choosing an Agent is trustworthiness. You need to choose someone who will follow your instructions and put the Power of Attorney to the use you intended. You need to choose someone, who, when using your Power of Attorney, will always put your interests ahead of his.

Perhaps you are less concerned with trustworthiness than the loss of your independence. You may want to give someone a Power of Attorney, but not until it is needed. This presents a dilemma. If you wait until it is needed, you may be too sick to sign the document. There are two simple solutions.

KEEP THE DOCUMENT IN YOUR POSSESSION

Before anyone (a bank, stockbroker, closing agent, etc.) will accept the Power of Attorney they will want to see the original document so that they are assured that your Attorney-In-Fact has authority to transact business on your behalf. If you keep the original document in your possession and do not give anyone a copy, your Attorney-In-Fact will not be able to act for you.

The only problem with this arrangement is that you need to arrange to make the document accessible to your Attorney-In-Fact in the event of your incapacity. If your Attorney-In-Fact is a trusted family member, you can tell him/her where the document is located, with instructions to take possession of the Durable Power of Attorney in the event of your incapacity.

Another solution may be to have your lawyer store the original document. You can have your lawyer draft your Power of Attorney so that it does not become effective until and unless you are too ill to manage your own affairs. You can give instructions to your lawyer to deliver the Financial Power of Attorney to your Attorney-In-Fact if and when your personal physician, and another independent physician, verify, in writing, that you are too ill to conduct your own business. You need to give a copy of such instructions to your Attorney-In-Fact, so that he can contact your lawyer and get possession of the document should the need ever arise.

USING THE POWER OF ATTORNEY FOR MEDICAL DECISIONS

Your attorney can design a Durable Power of Attorney, to meet your special needs. He can even include powers that relate to your health care. But as a practical matter, it may be better to have a separate document drafted to appoint a Health Care Agent. You may want a different person to serve as Health Care Agent. While all immediate family members may be excellent choices in making health care decisions, not all may be qualified to make a financial decision on your behalf.

Even if you want the same person to serve as Health Care Agent and Attorney-In-Fact for your finances, there is still the matter of privacy. Your Health Care Agent will give a copy of your Advance Directive to your physician to be placed in your medical file. Your doctors have no need to know of your business dealings; and vis-versa. To conduct business on your behalf your Attorney-In-Fact will need to give a copy of the Power of Attorney to your business associates (banks, stockbrokers, etc.). Your business associates have no need to know of your medical decisions. For privacy, and perhaps security reasons, consider having separate documents, rather than try to get it all into a single multi purpose document.

It is relatively simple and inexpensive to head off Guardianship proceedings. All you need do is appoint an Attorney-In-Fact under a Durable Power of Attorney to manage your finances, and a Health Care Agent under an Advance Directive to make your medical care decisions. These documents authorize people of your choice to care for you and your property in the event of your incapacity. But, despite your best plans, something unusual could happen causing a Court to decide that you in need of a Guardian. For example, suppose you disappear and cannot be found after a diligent search. It might be necessary to have a Court appoint a Guardian to protect your property in your absence (see Page 21). Or perhaps you develop an addiction or a mental illness causing self-destructive behavior. Your friends or family might decide that you are in need of protection and ask a Court to appoint a Guardian of your person.

Although it may not be possible to avoid all Guardianship proceedings, you can control who will be your Guardian by signing a document that states who you wish to serve as your Guardian in the event of your incapacity. You can have your attorney prepare a separate document, or you can include an appointment of your choice of Guardian of your person in your Advance Directive, and your choice of Guardian of your property in your Durable Power of Attorney. It is a good idea to nominate an alternate Guardian in the event that your first choice is unable or unwilling to serve as Guardian.

Should it be necessary to appoint a Guardian of your person or property, the Judge will give top priority to your choice of Guardian. If you do not appoint someone to serve as your Guardian, then Maryland statute establishes the following order of priority:

- 1st Your spouse
- 2nd Your parent
- 3rd Your adult son or daughter
- 4th Anyone entitled to inherit your property under Maryland's Laws of Intestate Succession
- 5th If you are being cared for by a public agency or other organization, then a person or corporation chosen by that agency or organization
- 6th If you are receiving benefits from a government agency, then a person or corporation chosen by that agency
- 7th Anyone chosen by the Court.

(Est. & Trusts 13-207, 13-707)

PROVIDING FOR LONG TERM CARE

The good news is: You are going to live longer.
The bad news is: It's going to cost you.

Scientists are doing a great job of prolonging life, but unless they find Ponce De Leon's fountain, the general population will age. Along with age comes infirmities. Eyes fail. Hearing diminishes. Nervous systems deteriorate. Digestive systems either speed up or slow down, all to the discomfort of the unhappy occupant of the body. It's all part of the "golden" years.

The pharmacology industry is well motivated to produce drugs that manage the ills associated with aging. Their research has led to a wealth of pharmaceutic products that do not cure, but do allow people to live relatively comfortably into advanced age. The only problem is the cost of these drugs. Medicare covers the treatment of life-threatening brushes with heart disease, stroke, cancer and diabetes; but, as of this writing, Medicare does not pay for maintenance medication that is often necessary once the condition is stabilized.

Medicare is also limited in long term health care coverage. It does not pay for extended nursing care. Medicare pays for the first 20 days of skilled nursing care. Medicare pays the excess over $99 for days 21 through 100. That means you pay $7,920 for the next 80 days. After 100 days, you are on your own. A nursing home stay of one or two years can wipe out the life savings of most working people. Once savings are gone, the government provides care in the form of Medicaid coverage.

If you are poor, long-term nursing care may not be of concern to you, because all your needs should be covered under Medicaid. If you are very wealthy, you may not worry because you have more than enough money to pay for your care. But the rest of us need to think about ways to provide for long-term health care. For those concerned about the loss of life savings because of illness, there is supplemental and/or long-term health care insurance. There are many different insurance plans available. You can call the National Association of Insurance Commissioners at (816) 842-3600 and they will forward to you, free of charge, the publication:

A SHOPPER'S GUIDE TO LONG TERM CARE INSURANCE

If you have a specific question, you can call the Maryland Department of Aging at (800) 243-3425.

FOR FEDERAL EMPLOYEES/RETIREES

The Long Term Care Security Act (Public Law 106-265) was passed by Congress to take effect in October, 2002. The law is designed to make long-term care insurance available to Federal employees, members of the uniformed services, and civilian and military retirees. The Office of Personnel Management is currently at work establishing the terms of the policy and determining the cost of the insurance policy to federal employees or retirees. You can download a copy of the law from their Web site:

OFFICE OF PERSONNEL MANAGEMENT
http://www.opm.gov/insure/ltc

The National Association Of Retired Federal Employees ("NARFE") has been actively involved in this new legislation. You can get updates on the law by calling their legislative hotline in Alexandria, Virginia at (703) 838-7780, or by visiting their Web site:

NARFE WEB SITE
http://www.narfe.org

Many people find themselves in the unhappy position of being uninsurable because of a pre-existing condition, or perhaps without sufficient income to pay for long term health insurance coverage. The worst case scenario is a person who has a serious illness and is too rich for Medicaid and too poor to afford nursing care without depleting their life savings.

People in this situation may decide to divest themselves of all property and hope that they will not need extended nursing care for at least three years. Once three years have passed, they hope to be eligible for Medicaid (MC 88A-65). For most, their motives are altruistic. The money is given to a child to keep safe for the parent, but what the parent is really trying to do is protect the child's inheritance.

The parent may rationalize "I worked all my life and hoped to leave a few pennies for the kids. Why did I work so hard? To give it all to a nursing home? Why should I use all of my life savings to pay for a few years of nursing care? Doesn't the government pay hundreds of thousands of dollars for people on Medicare to have open heart surgery, or to pay for lengthy and expensive cancer treatments? Why should people who suffer from the effects of a severe stroke, or from Alzheimer's or from Parkinsons not be entitled to receive similar benefits for their disease?"

And so they give all of their money away.

Giving away all assets and then waiting three years is what this author considers to be a "Brute Force" Medicaid Estate Plan. There's no finesse. It is a drastic step to take and fraught with perils. The obvious problems are ones we mentioned before when discussing the transfer of the homestead.

What if the child is sued?
What if the child gets married, or divorced?
What if the child falls on hard times?

But the real problem is the loss of independence. Being impoverished at a time in your life when you are unable to supplement your income, and when your physical health is declining, can lead to much sadness. Imagine going to your child and asking for money. Imagine the child thinking, or worse yet, asking,

"What is the money for?"

Before divesting yourself of your assets, or if you are the child, before you accept those assets, consult with an experienced Elder Law attorney. In many cases, there are other, better, strategies.

CAUTION Medicaid Estate Planning is a specialty. The attorney must know all of the federal and state laws relating to the subject. In addition, the attorney needs to know what strategies are liable to be challenged should the person need to apply for Medicaid. Before employing an attorney, determine what percentage of his practice is devoted to Medicaid Estate Planning and how long he has practiced in the field of Elder Law.

Your Estate Plan Record 11

Once you are satisfied with your Estate Plan, then the final thing to consider is whether your heirs will be able to locate your assets once you are deceased.

Most people have their business records in one place, their Will in another place, car titles and deeds in still another place. When someone dies, their beneficiaries may feel as if they are playing a game of "hide and seek" with the decedent. The game might be fun if it were not for the fact that things not found may be forever lost. For example, suppose you die in an accident and no one knows you are insured by your credit card company for accidental death in the amount of $25,000. The only one to profit is the insurance company, which is just that much richer because no one told them that you died as a result of an accident.

And how about a key to a safe deposit box located in another state? Will anyone find it? Even if they find the key, how will they find the box?

It is not difficult to arrange things so that your affairs are always in order. It amounts to being aware of what you own (and owe) and keeping a record of your possessions. A side benefit is that by doing so, you will always know where all your business records are. If you ever spent time trying to collect information to file your taxes or trying to find a lost stock or bond certificate, you will appreciate the value of organizing your records.

ORGANIZING YOUR RECORDS

Heirs need all the help they can get. It is difficult enough dealing with the loss, without the frustration of trying to locate important documents. Your heirs will have no problem locating your assets if you keep all of your records in a single place. It can be a desk drawer or a file cabinet or even a shoe box. It is helpful if you keep a separate file or folder for each type of investment. You might consider setting up the following folders:

THE BANK & SECURITIES FOLDER

Store your original certificates for stocks, bonds, mutual funds, certificates of deposit, in a folder labeled BANK & SECURITIES FOLDER. In addition to the original certificate include a copy of the contract you signed with each financial institution. The contract will show where you have funds and who you named as beneficiary or joint owner of the account. If someone owes you money and has signed a Promissory note or mortgage that identifies you as the lender, then you can store these documents in this folder as well.

If you wish to store your original documents in a safe deposit box, then keep a record of the location of the safe deposit box, and the number of the box, in this folder. Make a copy of all of the items stored in the box and place the copies in this folder. If you have an extra key to the box, then put the key in the folder. If you are the only person with access to the box, it may take a Probate procedure to remove items from the box once you die. Consider allowing someone you trust to be able to gain entry to the box in the event of your incapacity or death.

THE INSURANCE FOLDER

The INSURANCE FOLDER is for each original insurance policy that you own, be it car insurance, homeowner's insurance or a health care insurance policy. If you purchased real property, you probably received a title commitment at closing and the original title insurance policy some weeks later when you received your original deed from recording. If you cannot locate the title insurance policy, then contact the closing agent and have them send you a copy of your title policy.

THE PENSION AND ANNUITY FOLDER

If you have a Pension or Annuity, then put all of the documents relating to the Pension in this folder. Include the telephone number and/or address of the person to contact in the event of your death.

FOR FEDERAL RETIREES If you are a Federal Retiree, you should have received your **P**ERSONAL **I**DENTIFICATION **N**UMBER **(PIN)** and the person who will inherit your pension (your ***survivor annuitant***) should have received his/her own PIN as well. It is relatively simple to obtain this during your lifetime, but it may be difficult and/or stressful for your survivor annuitant to work through the system once you are gone.

Survivor annuitant benefits are not automatic. Your survivor annuitant must apply for them by submitting a death claim to the Office of Personnel Management. Your survivor needs to know that it is necessary to apply and also how to apply. You can get printed information about how apply for benefits from the Office Of Personnel Management (see Page 30). Keep the printed information in this file.

THE DEED FOLDER

Many people save every scrap of paper associated with the closing of real property. If you closed recently on real estate and there was a mortgage involved in the purchase, you probably walked away from closing with enough paper to wallpaper your kitchen. If you wish, you can keep all of those papers in a separate file that identifies the property, for example:

CLOSING PAPERS FOR THE BALTIMORE CONDO

Set aside the original deed (or a copy if the original is in a safe deposit box) and place it into a separate DEED FOLDER. Include deeds to parcels of real property, cemetery deeds, condominium deeds, cooperative shares to real property, timesharing certificates, etc. Include deeds to out of state property as well as Maryland property in the DEED FOLDER. If you have a mortgage on your property, then put a copy of the mortgage and promissory note in a separate LIABILITY FOLDER.

LOCATING REAL PROPERTY

If you own a vacant lot, your beneficiaries will find the deed (or a copy) in this folder but that deed will not contain the address of that property because it doesn't have one. The post office does not assign a street address until someone actually lives at the site. Your beneficiary could get the location of the property from city or county records. But why make things hard for them? Include a simple handwritten note in this folder that tells them exactly how to locate the property.

THE LIABILITY FOLDER

The LIABILITY FOLDER should contain all loan documents of debts that you owe. For example, if you purchased real property and have a mortgage on that property, then put a copy of the mortgage and promissory note in this folder. If you owe money on a car, put the promissory note and chattel mortgage on the car in the file. If you have a credit card, put a copy of the contract you signed with the credit card company in this file. Many people never take the time to calculate their net worth (what a person owns less what that person owes). By having a record of your assets and outstanding debts, you can calculate your net worth whenever you wish.

THE ESTATE PLANNING DOCUMENT FOLDER

Place your Will and/or Trust in a separate folder. If the original document is in a safe deposit box or with your attorney, then place a copy of the document into this folder together with instructions about how to find the original. If you placed your Will with the Register of Wills, then include the receipt for the Will, and the address of the Probate Court, in the folder.

THE PERSONAL PROPERTY FOLDER

MOTOR VEHICLES Put all motor vehicle titles in a Personal Property folder. This includes cars, mobile homes, boats, planes, etc. If you owe money on the vehicle, the lender may have possession of the title certificate. If such is the case, then put a copy of the title certificate and registration in this folder and a copy of the promissory note or chattel mortgage in a separate liability folder. If you have a boat or plane, then identify the location of the motor vehicle. For example, if you are leasing space in an airplane hanger or in a marina, keep a copy of the leasing agreement in this file.

JEWELRY If you own expensive jewelry, keep a picture of the item together with the sales receipt or written appraisal in this folder.

COLLECTOR'S ITEMS If you own a valuable art or coin collection, or any other item of significant value, include a picture of the item in this file. Also include evidence of ownership of the item, such as a sales receipt or a certificate of authenticity, or a written appraisal of the property.

THE PERSONAL RECORD FOLDER

The PERSONAL RECORD FOLDER should include documents that relate to you personally, such as a birth certificate, naturalization papers, pre-nuptial or post- nuptial agreement, marriage certificate, divorce papers, army records, social security card; etc. If you have an Advance Directive or a Power of Attorney, then this is a good place for these documents. If you placed the original document in a safe deposit box, then keep a copy in this folder together with the location of the original.

THE TAX RECORD FOLDER

Your Personal Representative (or next of kin) will need to file your final income tax returns. Keep a copy of your tax returns (both Federal and state) for the past three years in your Tax Record Folder.

CAPITAL GAINS RECORD

As explained on page 38, as of 2010, there will be a cap on the step-up basis of inherited property of 4.3 million for property inherited by the spouse and 1.3 million for everyone else. It is important that you keep a careful record of the basis of your property, not only for your heirs, but yourself should you decide to sell the property during your lifetime. If you purchase a stock, then you need to keep a record of the money you paid for that stock. If you purchase real property, then you need to keep a record of the purchase price as well as monies you paid to improve the property. Your accountant can help you set up a bookkeeping system to keep a running record of your basis in everything you own of value.

Many do not have the time, nor inclination, to "play" with all these folders. They do not anticipate an immediate demise. Getting hit by a truck, or dying in a fiery plane crash is not something to think about, much less prepare for. But consider that death is not the only problem. You could take suddenly ill (say with a stroke) and become incapacitated. Even the most time-starved optimist should have a murmur of concern that their loved ones will be left with a mess should something unforeseen happen.

If you do not feel like doing a complete job of organizing your records at this time, consider an abridged version. You can set up a single file with a list of all you own and the location of each item. You need to make that file easily accessible to whoever you wish to manage your affairs in the event of your incapacity or death. You can do this by letting that person know of the existence of the file and how to get it in an emergency; or keep the file in an easily accessed place in your home with the succinct but attention-grabbing title of "***If I Die***."

We have included a form on the next page that you can use as a basis for information to be included in the file.

If I Die

then the following information will help settle my estate:

INFORMATION FOR DEATH CERTIFICATE

MY FULL LEGAL NAME ____________________
MY SOCIAL SECURITY NO. ____________________
MY USUAL OCCUPATION ____________________
BIRTH DATE AND BIRTH PLACE ____________________
If naturalized, date & place ____________________
MY FATHER'S NAME ____________________
MY MOTHER'S MAIDEN NAME ____________________

PERSONS TO BE NOTIFIED OF MY DEATH

____
____
____

FUNERAL AND BURIAL ARRANGEMENTS

LOCATION OF BURIAL SITE

____

LOCATION OF PRENEED FUNERAL CONTRACT

____

FOR VETERAN or SPOUSE BURIAL IN A NATIONAL CEMETERY

BRANCH____________________SERIAL NO.____________________
VETERAN'S RANK ____________________
VETERAN'S VA CLAIM NUMBER ____________________
DATE AND PLACE OF ENTRY INTO SERVICE:

____

DATE AND PLACE OF SEPARATION FROM SERVICE:

____

LOCATION OF OFFICIAL MILITARY DISCHARGE
OR DD 214 FORM____________________

LOCATION OF LEGAL DOCUMENTS

BIRTH CERTIFICATE ______________________________

MARRIAGE CERTIFICATE ______________________________

DIVORCE DECREE ______________________________

PASSPORT ______________________________

WILL OR TRUST ______________________________

DEEDS ______________________________

MORTGAGES ______________________________

TITLE TO MOTOR VEHICLES ______________________________

ADVANCE DIRECTIVE ______________________________

POWER OF ATTORNEY ______________________________

Name, telephone of attorney ______________________________

LOCATION OF FINANCIAL RECORDS

INSURANCE POLICIES:

Name of Company, Location of Policy, Insurance Agent

____

____

PENSIONS/ANNUITIES:

IF FEDERAL RETIREE: PIN NUMBER: ______________________________

NAME OF SURVIVOR ______________________________

SURVIVOR PIN NUMBER ______________________________

BANK

Name and address of Bank, Account Number,
Location of Safe Deposit Box and Key

____

____

SECURITIES

Name and telephone number of broker

____

TAX RECORDS FOR PAST 3 YEARS

LOCATION ______________________________

Name and telephone number of accountant

____

WHEN TO UPDATE YOUR ESTATE PLAN

We discussed people's natural disinclination to make an Estate Plan until they are faced with their own mortality. Many believe that they will make just one Will and then die (maybe that's why they put off making a Will). The reality is, most people who make a Will change it at least once before they die. If you have an Estate Plan, it is important to update it when any of the following events take place:

✍ CHANGE IN MARITAL STATUS

If you are married or divorced, there are certain changes in your Estate Plan that take place by law. For example, if you have a Will and then get married and have a child, then that Will is automatically revoked by Maryland law. Similarly, if you divorce and then die before you get around to changing a Will that you made during your marriage, then any provision that you made in your Will for your ex-spouse will be read as if your ex-spouse died before you (Est. & Trusts 4-105). But it is important to not just rely on the law. Best to change all documents after a marriage, divorce or separation. This includes Advance Directives, Powers of Attorney, deeds, pension plans, insurance policies, etc.

NOTIFY EMPLOYER OF CHANGE IN RELATIONSHIP

If you change your marital status (either marry or divorce) you need to tell your employer of the change so that the employer can change your status for purposes of health insurance coverage.

✍ A CHANGE IN RELATIONSHIP

If you get married, divorced, have a child, or a beneficiary of your estate dies, then you should examine your Estate Plan to determine whether it needs to be revised. If you decide that your Will needs to be completely revised, then it is important to have a new Will prepared. Ripping up the old Will effectively revokes it (Est. & Trusts 4-105). But it could happen that someone (perhaps your attorney) has a copy of the Will. If no one knows that you revoked the Will, they may think the Will is lost and then offer the copy of the Will for Probate (see page 75). If you draft a new Will, then the first paragraph should say, "I revoke all prior Wills ..." and there will be no question that the new Will is the way you want your Estate to be settled.

BENEFICIARY MOVES OR DIES

Most people remember to name an alternate beneficiary should a beneficiary die during ones lifetime. But how many of us remember to notify the pension plan or insurance company of a change of address? It is important that your beneficiary's address be available to those in charge of distributing funds upon your death. Many insurance policies are never paid because the company cannot locate the beneficiary. In 1998, the Office of Federal Employees' Group Life Insurance reported that they had 29 million dollars in unpaid benefits, mostly because the beneficiary could not be located at their last given address.

✍ RELOCATION TO A NEW STATE OR COUNTRY

There is no need to change your Estate Plan for a move within the state of Maryland. If you changed your county of residence and you deposited your original Will with the Register of Wills, then you need to retrieve that Will and deposit it with the Register in the county of your new residence. If you move to a new state, then you need to retrieve your Will from the Register of Wills and take it with you to the new state. Not every state allows the deposit of a Will prior to the death of the Will maker. You may need to make other arrangements to store your Will in the new state.

There is much to check out for a move to another state or country. Each state (and country) has its own laws relating to the inheritance of property and those laws are very different from each other. The rights of a spouse to inherit property varies significantly from state to state. There is a world of difference between the rights of a spouse in a community property state and other states. And there is even variation in the rights of a spouse from one community property state to another!

If you have a Will or Trust, and you are married, you need to check with an attorney to be sure that your Will or Trust cannot be challenged in the new state because you did not leave your spouse the minimum amount required by the laws of that state.

You also need to check out the taxes of the new state. Each state has its own estate tax structure. Some states have an inheritance tax or a transfer tax on all inherited property. If state taxes are high, you may need an Estate Plan that will minimize the impact of those taxes. Creditor protection is another item that is significantly different state to state. If you have much debt, then determine what items can be inherited by your family free of your debts.

Each state has its own, unique, laws of Intestate Succession. Who has the right to inherit your property in the state of Maryland may be different from who can inherit your property in another state. If you do not have a Will, then this is the time to think about who will get your property in the state of your residence.

If you have an Advance Directive or a Power of Attorney, then you need to determine whether these documents will be honored in the new state. Laws relating to Health Care vary significantly. Other states may no laws providing for the appointment of a Health Care Agent, but they may have laws that enable you to appoint a Patient Advocate or a Health Care Surrogate with the right to make your health care decisions in the event that you are too ill to do so yourself. It is best to sign a new health care document using the form recognized in that state, rather than chance any confusion should you become ill and find yourself in an emergency situation.

When moving to another state you need to either educate yourself about the laws of the state, or to consult with an attorney who can assist you in reviewing your Estate Plan to see if that plan will accomplish your goals in that state.

✍ A SIGNIFICANT CHANGE IN THE LAW

We pay our legislators (state and federal) to make laws and, if necessary, change those in effect. We pay judges to interpret the law and that interpretation may change the way the law operates. The legislature and the judiciary do their job and so laws change frequently. Tax laws are particularly volatile. The 2001 change in the tax law not only changed income taxes, it significantly increased the Exclusion amount so that by 2010 no Estate Tax will be due regardless of the value of your Estate. You may be thinking that there is no need for an Estate Tax plan because you don't intend to die prior to 2010. But any certainty relating to death and taxes is false security (especially taxes, in this case). As explained in Chapter 8, the law as passed in 2001, is effective only until December 31, 2010. If lawmakers do nothing, then in 2011, the federal Estate Tax goes back into effect; and estates that exceed one million dollars will once again be subject to Estate taxes.

And that is not the only uncertainty. Each state has its own Estate Tax structure. It remains to be seen how each state will react to the Federal change. Some states may follow the lead of the Federal government and increase their Estate Tax exclusion in the same manner. Other states may see this as an opportunity to "pick up the slack" i.e., to increase their Estate Taxes, so that monies that would have been paid to the Federal government will now be paid to the state.

You need to keep up with the news to learn about changes in the law that affect your Estate Plan. It is a good idea to check with your attorney on a regular basis to see if any change in the state or Federal law affects your current Estate plan. And also check out the Eagle Web site for changes we will post to keep this book fresh:

http://www.eaglepublishing.com

GAMES DECEDENTS PLAY

We discussed the game of "hide and seek" some decedents play with their heirs. A variation of that game is the "wild goose chase." The person who plays this game is one who never updates his files. His records are filled with all sorts of lapsed insurance policies, promissory notes of debts long since paid; brokerage statements of securities that have been sold, and so on.

When he is gone, his family will become frustrated as they try to hunt down the "missing" asset. If you wish to play this game, then the best joke is to keep the key to a safe deposit box that you are no longer leasing. That will keep folks hunting for a long time!

If you do not have a wicked sense of humor, then do your family a favor and update your records on a regular basis.

Glossary

ADMINISTRATION The ***administration*** of a Probate Estate is the management and settlement of the decedent's affairs. There are different types of administration. See ***Ancillary Administration and Modified administration.***

ADVANCE DIRECTIVE An ***Advance Directive*** is a written, notarized statement, in which the person (the ***principal***) signing the document appoints a ***Health Care Agent*** to carry out the directions given in the Advance Directive in the event the Principal is too ill to speak for himself. See ***Living Will***.

AFFIANT An ***affiant*** is someone who signs an affidavit and swears or acknowledges that it is true in the presence of a Notary Public or other person with authority to administer an oath or take acknowledgments.

AFFIDAVIT An ***affidavit*** is a written statement of fact made by someone voluntarily, under oath, or acknowledged as being true, in the presence of a notary public or someone else who has authority to administer an oath or take acknowledgments.

AGENT An ***agent*** is someone who is authorized by another (the principal) to act for or in place of the principal.

ANATOMICAL GIFT An ***anatomical gift*** is the donation of all or part of the body of the decedent for a specified purpose, such as transplantation or research.

ANCILLARY ADMINISTRATION An ***ancillary administration*** is a probate procedure that aids or assists the original (primary) probate proceeding. Ancillary administration is conducted in another state to determine the beneficiary of the decedent's property located within that state, and to determine whether the property is taxable in that state.

ANNUITANT An ***annuitant*** is someone who is entitled to receive payments under an annuity contract.

ANNUITY An ***annuity*** is a contract that gives someone (the annuitant) the right to receive periodic payments (monthly, quarterly) either for life or for a number of years.

ASSET An ***asset*** is anything owned by someone that has a value, including personal property (jewelry, paintings, securities, cash, motor vehicles, etc.) and real property (condominiums, vacant lots, acreage, residences, etc.)

BENEFICIARY A ***beneficiary*** is one who benefits from the act of another or from the transfer of property. In this book we refer to a beneficiary as someone named in a Will or Trust to receive property, or someone who inherits property under the Laws of Intestate Succession.

BY REPRESENTATION ***By Representation*** is a method of distributing a gift, in equal shares, to a group of people such that if one of them dies before the gift is made, then the deceased person's share goes to his/her lineal descendants.

CAVEAT ***Caveat*** is Latin for "Let him beware." It is a warning for the reader to be careful.

CHARITABLE REMAINDER ANNUITY TRUST A ***Charitable Remainder Annuity Trust*** is a Trust that is required to pay an annuity to a designated person for a certain period of time. Once the annuity is paid, whatever remains in the Trust is donated to a tax exempt charity.

CIRCUIT A ***circuit*** is a judicial division. The state of Maryland is divided into 8 judicial circuits each with its own ***Circuit Court***. Each judicial circuit covers one or more county, with the exception of the 8th Circuit which just covers Baltimore City.

CLAIM A ***Claim*** against the decedent's estate is a demand for payment of a debt of the decedent. To be effective, the claim must be filed with the Probate court within the time limits set by law.

CODE A ***Code*** is a body of laws arranged systematically for easy reference e.g. the Internal Revenue Code.

COLUMBARIUM A ***Columbarium*** is a vault with niches (spaces) for urns that contain the ashes of cremated bodies.

COMMON LAW MARRIAGE A ***Common Law marriage*** is one that is entered into without a state marriage license nor any kind of official marriage ceremony. A common law marriage is created by an agreement to marry, followed by the two living together as man and wife. Most states do not recognize a common law marriage.

COURT The ***Court*** as used in this book is the Court that handles Probate matters (see Orphan's Court and Circuit Court). When referring to an order made by the court then the term is synonymous with "judge," i.e., an "order of the court" is an order made by the judge of the court.

CREMAINS The word ***Cremains*** is an abbreviation of the term ***cremated remains***. It is also referred to as the ***ashes*** of a person who has been cremated.

CURTESY ***Curtesy*** is the right of a husband, upon the death of his wife, to a life estate in real property she owned during their marriage, provided they had a surviving child who could inherit the property. This English Common Law has been abolished in most states, including Maryland.

DAMAGES ***Damages*** is money that is awarded by a Court as compensation to someone who has been injured by the action of another.

DECEDENT The ***Decedent*** is the person who died.

DESCENDANT A ***Descendant*** is someone who descends from a common ancestor. There are two kinds of descendants: a *lineal descendant* and a *collateral descendant*. The lineal descendant is one who descends in a straight line such as father to son to grandson. The collateral descendant is one who descends in a parallel line, such as a cousin. In this book, unless otherwise stated, the term *descendant* refers to a *lineal descendant*.

DISTRIBUTION The ***distribution*** of a trust estate or of a Probate Estate is the giving or transferring to a beneficiary that part of the estate to which the beneficiary is entitled.

D.I.Y. Do It Yourself.

DOWER ***Dower*** is the right of a wife, upon the death of her husband, to a life estate in 1/3rd of all real property that he during their marriage. This English Common Law has been abolished in most states, including Maryland.

DURABLE POWER OF ATTORNEY A ***Durable Power of Attorney*** is a document in which the person who signs the document (the ***Principal***) gives another person (his ***Attorney in Fact***) authority to do certain things on behalf of the Principal. The Attorney in Fact is also referred to as the Principal's ***Agent***. The word ***"durable"*** means that the authority of the Agent continues even if the Principal is incapacitated at the time that the Agent is acting on behalf of the Principal.

ESTATE A person's ***Estate*** is all of the property (both real and personal property) owned by that person. The decedent's estate may also be referred to as his ***Taxable Estate*** because all of the decedent's assets must be included when determining whether any Estate taxes are due after the person dies. Compare to Probate Estate.

FIDUCIARY A ***Fiduciary*** is one who holds property in trust for another, or one who acts for the benefit of another, such as a Personal Representative, Trustee, Guardian etc.

FRATERNAL BENEFIT SOCIETY A ***Fraternal Benefit Society*** is a not for profit society or voluntary association that is organized for the mutual benefit of its members and to work together to accomplish some worthy goal.

GRANTEE The ***Grantee*** (also called the party of the second part) named in a deed is the person who receives title to the property from the grantor.

GRANTOR A ***Grantor*** is someone who transfers property. The grantor of a deed is the person who transfers property to a new owner (the ***Grantee***). The grantor of a trust is someone who creates the trust and then transfer's property into the trust. See ***Settlor***.

GUARDIAN A ***Guardian*** is someone who has legal authority to care for the person or property of a minor or for someone who has been found by the court to be incapacitated.

HEALTH CARE AGENT A ***Health Care Agent*** is someone who is appointed by another (the ***Principal)*** to make medical decisions on behalf of the Principal, in the event that the Principal is to too ill to speak for himself.

HEIR An ***Heir*** is anyone entitled to inherit the decedent's property under the Laws of Descent and Distribution in the event that the decedent dies without a Will.

HOMESTEAD The ***homestead*** is the dwelling and land owned and occupied as the owner's principal residence.

INCAPACITATED A person is ***incapacitated*** if he/she lacks sufficient understanding or ability to make or to communicate responsible decisions for himself/herself. If a court finds that a person is a person is incapacitated because of age or a physical condition, then the court will appoint someone to care for person or property of the incapacitated person.

INDIGENT A person who is ***indigent*** is one who is poor and without funds.

INTESTATE ***Intestate*** means not having a Will or dying without a Will. ***Testate*** is to have a Will or dying with a Will.

IRREVOCABLE CONTRACT An ***irrevocable contract*** is a contract that cannot be revoked, withdrawn, or cancelled by any of the parties to that contract.

IRREVOCABLE INSURANCE TRUST An ***Irrevocable Insurance Trust*** is a Trust that is set up to purchase life insurance. The insured person is not the beneficiary nor the owner of the policy. The Trust is the owner of the policy. The proceeds of the life insurance policy go to the beneficiary of the Trust free of the claims of the creditors of the insured person.

JOINT AND SEVERAL LIABILITY If two or more people agree to be ***jointly and severally liable*** to pay a debt, then each individually agree to be responsible to pay the debt, and together they all agree to pay for the debt.

KEY MAN INSURANCE ***Key man insurance*** is an insurance policy designed to protect a company from economic loss in the event that an important employee of the company becomes disabled or dies.

LEGALESE ***Legalese*** refers to the use of legal terms and confusing text that is used by some attorneys to draft legal documents.

LETTERS ***Letters*** is a document, issued by the Probate court, giving the Personal Representative authority to take possession of and to administer the estate of the decedent.

LIEN A ***Lien*** is a charge against a person's property as security for a debt. The lien is evidence of the creditor's right to take the property as full or partial payment, in the event that the debtor defaults in paying the monies owed.

LIFE ESTATE A ***Life Estate*** interest in real property is the right to possess and occupy that property for so long as the holder of the life estate lives.

LINEAL DESCENDANT A ***Lineal Descendant*** of the decedent is someone who is his direct descendant, such as his child, grandchild, great-grandchild etc.

LITIGATION ***Litigation*** is the process of carrying on a lawsuit, i.e., to sue for some right or remedy in a court of law. A Litigation Attorney is one who is experienced in conducting the law suit and in particular, going to trial.

LIVING WILL A ***Living Will*** is a Health Care Directive that gives instructions about whether life support systems should be withheld in the event that the person who signs the Living Will is terminally ill or in a persistent vegetative state and unable to speak for himself.

MODIFIED ADMINISTRATION A ***Modified Administration*** is an abridged Probate procedure that is available if the only beneficiaries are the decedent's spouse, child, or Personal Representative.

MEDICAID ***Medicaid*** is a public assistance program sponsored jointly by the federal and state government to provide medical care for people with low income.

NET ESTATE The ***Net Estate*** is the decedent's Probate Estate less all valid bills and taxes, but not the Inheritance Tax which is paid for by whomever actually inherits the property (Est. & Trusts 3-102).

NET PROCEEDS The ***net proceeds*** of a sale is the sale price less costs and expenses paid to make the sale.

NET WORTH A person's ***net worth*** is the value of all of the property that he owns less the monies he owes.

NEXT OF KIN ***Next of kin*** has two meanings in law: ***next of kin*** can refer to a person's nearest blood relation or it can refer to those people (not necessarily blood relations) who are entitled to inherit the property of the decedent if the decedent died without a will.

ORPHAN'S COURT In most counties in Maryland, Probate procedures are conducted in the ***Orphan's Court***. In Montgomery and Harford counties, a Judge in the Circuit Court handles Probate matters.

PERJURY ***Perjury*** is lying under oath. The false statement can be made as a witness in court or by signing an Affidavit. Perjury is a criminal offense.

PERSONAL PROPERTY ***Personal property*** is all property owned by a person that is not real property (real estate). It includes cars, stocks, house furnishings, jewelry, etc.

PERSONAL REPRESENTATIVE A ***Personal Representative*** is someone who is appointed by the Probate court to settle the decedent's estate and to distribute whatever is left to the proper beneficiary.

PETITION A ***Petition*** is a formal written request to a Court asking the Court to take action or issue an order on a given matter.

POST-NUPTIAL AGREEMENT A ***Post-nuptial agreement*** is an agreement made by a couple after marriage to decide their respective rights in case of a dissolution or the death of a spouse

POWER OF ATTORNEY A ***Power of Attorney*** is a document in which the person who signs the document (the ***Principal***) gives another person (his ***Attorney-In-Fact***) or ***Agent***) authority to do certain things on behalf of the Principal.

PRE-NUPTIAL AGREEMENT A ***Pre-nuptial agreement*** (also known as an ***Antenuptial agreement***) is an agreement made prior to marriage whereby a couple determines how their property is to be managed during their marriage and how their property is to be divided should one die, or they later divorce.

PROBATE ***Probate*** is a court procedure in which a court determines the existence of a valid Will and then supervises the distribution of the Probate Estate of the decedent.

PROBATE ESTATE The ***Probate Estate*** is that part of the decedent's estate that is subject to probate. It includes property that the decedent owned in his name only. It does not include property that was jointly held by the decedent and someone else. It does not include property held "in trust for" or "for the benefit of" someone.

REAL PROPERTY ***Real property,*** also known as ***real estate,*** is land and anything permanently attached to the land such as buildings and fences.

REGISTER OF WILLS The ***Register Of Wills*** is a public office established under the Constitution of Maryland. Each county and Baltimore City has an Office of the Register of Wills. It is the job of the Register of Wills to assist people who are preparing forms for Probate.

RESIDENT AGENT A ***Resident Agent*** of a corporation is someone who is authorized to act on behalf of the company and accept service of process in the event the company is sued.

RESIDUARY BENEFICIARY A ***residuary beneficiary*** is a beneficiary named in a Will who is entitled to whatever is left of the Probate Estate once the specific gifts made in the Will have been distributed and once the decedent's bills, taxes and costs of probate have been paid. If there is more than one residuary beneficiary, then they share equally in the residuary estate.

SETTLOR A ***Settlor*** is someone who furnishes property that is placed in a Trust. If the Settlor is also the creator of the Trust, then the Settlor is also referred to as the Grantor.

SLANDER ***Slander*** is making a false and malicious statement that prejudices a person's reputation or business.

SPENDTHRIFT A ***Spendthrift*** is someone who spends money carelessly or wastefully or extravagantly.

SPENDTHRIFT TRUST A ***Spendthrift Trust*** is a trust created to provide monies to a beneficiary, and at the same time protect the beneficiary from the monies from being taken by the his creditors.

STATUTE OF LIMITATION A ***Statute of Limitation*** is a federal or state law that sets maximum time periods for taking legal action. Once the time set out in the statute passes, no legal action can be taken.

TENANCY BY THE ENTIRETY A ***Tenancy by the Entirety*** is the name of a form of ownership of real property held by a husband and wife. It has the same legal effect as a joint tenancy with right of survivorship.

TENANCY IN COMMON ***Tenancy in common*** is a form of ownership such that each tenant owns his/her share without any claim to that share by the other tenants. Unlike a joint tenancy, there is no right of survivorship. Once a tenant in common dies, his/her share belongs to the tenant's estate and not to the remaining owners of the property.

TESTATE ***Testate*** means having a Will or dying with a Will.

TITLE INSURANCE ***Title Insurance*** is a policy issued by a title company after searching title to the property. The policy insures the accuracy of the title search against a claim of a defective title.

TRUST AGREEMENT A ***Trust Agreement*** is document in which someone (the Grantor or Trustor) creates a trust and appoints a trustee to manage property placed into the trust. The usual purpose of the trust is to benefit persons or charities named by the Grantor as beneficiaries of the trust.

TRUSTEE A ***Trustee*** is a person, or institution, who accepts the duty of caring for property for the benefit of another.

UNDUE INFLUENCE ***Undue influence*** is pressure, influence or persuasion that overpowers a person's free will or judgment, so that a person acts according to the will or purpose of the dominating party.

VOID MARRIAGE A ***void marriage*** is a marriage that has no legal effect in the state. The state does not recognize the marriage as being valid. Neither partner has the right to inherit under the state's Laws of Intestate Succession. Neither partner can request a divorce, because the state does not consider the couple to be married.

WAIVER A ***waiver*** is the intentional and voluntary giving up of a known right.

WARD A ***Ward*** is a minor or an incapacitated person who is placed by the Court under the care and supervision of a Guardian.

WARRANTY DEED A ***warranty deed*** is a deed in which someone (the Grantor) transfers the property to another (the Grantee) and guarantees good title, i.e., the Grantor guarantees that he has the right to transfer the property, and that no one else has any right to the property.

WRONGFUL DEATH A ***wrongful death*** is a death that was caused by the willful or negligent act of a person or company.

INDEX

D

E

T

U

V

W

SEE NEXT PAGE FOR
MARYLAND WEB SITES

170 Maryland Statutes are referenced in

Guiding Those Left Behind In Maryland

Each state has its own set of laws relating to the settlement of a person's estate. The Maryland laws that are referenced in this book are very different from the laws of other states. The author is in now in the process of "translating" *Guiding Those Left Behind . . .* for the rest of the states; that is, to write a book that incorporates the laws of the state into a book that describes how to settle the affairs of a decedent in that state, and how to prepare an estate plan that is appropriate for the state.

Arizona, California, Florida, Georgia, Illinois, Indiana, Maryland, Massachusetts, Michigan, New Jersey, New York, North Carolina, Ohio, Pennsylvania, Tennessee, Texas, Virginia, Washington and Wisconsin are now in print. The following books are scheduled for release in December, 2001:

Guiding Those Left Behind In Alabama
Guiding Those Left Behind In Colorado
Guiding Those Left Behind In Minnesota
Guiding Those Left Behind In Missouri
Guiding Those Left Behind In South Carolina

To order a book call (800) 824-0823.

Visit our Web site http://www.eaglepublishing.com to check whether books for other states are available at this time.

Beyond Grief To Acceptance and Peace

AMELIA E. POHL and the noted psychologist BARBARA J. SIMMONDS, Ph.d, have written a book for those families who have suffered a loss.

Beyond Grief To Acceptance and Peace explains:

- What to say to the bereaved
- How to help a child through the loss
- Strategies to adjust to a new lifestyle
- When and where to seek assistance.

The second edition of this 80 page book is now available for $9.95 plus shipping and handling. You can order the book using the following discount coupon for a total of $9.